Can't Trump This 2017
Top Trump Wins & Epic Speeches

Ed Martin
President, Phyllis Schlafly Eagles

Print ISBN 978-0-9984000-7-5

Skellig
AMERICA

TABLE OF CONTENTS

Dedication

To President Donald J. Trump

and

To Phyllis Schlafly (1924-2016):
the indispensable woman of America who,
with her love for her fellow man,
her heartfelt knowledge of America's greatness,
and her impeccable political judgment,
made America great again.

With the gratitude of a grateful nation.

For more on Phyllis and her life, please visit www.PhyllisSchlafly.com

"We're going to win so much, you're going to get tired of winning. You're going to say: 'Please, Mr. President, I have a headache. Please, don't win so much. This is getting terrible.' And I'm going to say, 'No, we have to make America great again.' You're gonna say, 'Please.' I'll say: 'Nope, nope. We're gonna keep winning'."

Donald J. Trump, February 2016

"[W]e are winning. We're winning again. We're winning a lot bigger than anyone ever thought possible for such a short period of time."

Donald J. Trump, November 30, 2017, St. Charles, Missouri

Preface

Election Night 2016 proved to be disconcerting for many in Washington, D.C. It dismayed some, surprised many, but absolutely shocked to the core those inhabiting the salons of power. Few, if any, believed that Donald Trump could win. From Wall Street to K Street and Madison Avenue to Pennsylvania Avenue, elites of all stripes viewed Trump's campaign as a lark and dismissed it as they prepared to deal with a second President Clinton.

In the backroom, political realm, Never Trump Republicans looked ahead and readied themselves for a 2020 campaign while their Democratic counterparts jockeyed for Clinton administration jobs. On K Street— truthfully, throughout the world—big money interests began plotting how to pay off the Clinton Foundation, the Podestas, and other Clinton global gatekeepers. In the media, one top TV executive told me that he and his colleagues had not ever entertained the thought of "President Trump" until about 8:30pm on November 8 as the numbers started to shift from what many had viewed as the inevitable to what now seemed unthinkable.

Their shock at Trump's election carried over into 2017. The same people who had refused to believe that Trump could win struggle, even today, to accept or believe that The Donald governs from the historic Oval Office. When asked about Trump's substantive achievements, they deny the very premise of the question, refusing to recognize all that he has accomplished in his first year in office.

Over and over, I meet people who do not believe—or, more correctly, will not believe—how much President Trump has actually done in his mission of making America great again. Instead, their heads seem to resonate with the battered media mantra, "Russia! Twitter! Charlottesville!" In doing so, they fail to appreciate, or even bear witness, to the beginning of a great and truly historic presidency.

To my ongoing surprise, far too many Trump supporters remain bruised and beaten down by those stale media chants. They wonder if the slow pace of change is an indication that, perhaps, Trump has fallen short. They do not need a pep talk or a support group. They simply need a reminder.

This book provides just such a resource. Because, when all has been said and done, when the policies have been examined, tested, and analyzed, and when the history books have been written, Trump friends and foes alike will look back with certainty at 2017 and share one basic truth about Trump's freshman year in the West Wing of 1600 ... you can't Trump this.

Merry Christmas!

Ed Martin
Phyllis Schlafly Center
St. Louis, Missouri
December 25, 2017

Foreword by Stephen K. Bannon

Victory begets victory.

America is in an epic war for its survival as a Republic and the principles upon which it was founded. We have come off-track in the years since the fall of the Soviet Union and we are now a crisis of the Judeo-Christian West, a crisis of capitalism, a crisis of our culture.

The presidential election of Donald J. Trump was a pivotal battle in this war, an aggressive blitz against those in the Swamp—the global elites, media, GOP establishment, and the Democrats and their progressive vanguard.

Donald J. Trump planted the flag to Make America Great Again during the campaign, the Trump Miracle happened, and he is now delivering. Big league.

To get to this point was no easy task, and to get to where we need to be will be even more difficult. We need to understand how to win. Nothing else matters in our polity. We need to get out of bed every day, roll up our sleeves and fight as citizens for the principles that make our Republic great.

History will record in the bleakest hours Phyllis Schlafly was one of America's most important fighters for freedom. Phyllis and Mr. Trump had struck up an unlikely friendship: the brash New York billionaire and this First Lady of American conservatism. Over the course of the campaign, they and their staffs had been in frequent contact and Mr. Trump's success on key issues and campaign style were influenced by Phyllis. Phyllis wrote about Mr. Trump and his policies over 50 times during the campaign and laid down a drumbeat of why he was the right man for the job. Her New York Times best-selling "The Conservative Case for Trump," released the day after her death on September 5, 2016, helped get and hold the conservative evangelicals and pro-life Catholics we so desperately needed.

And Phyllis' great work was aided by her confidante and protégé, Ed Martin.

Ed Martin is a one of the most respected grass roots leader in America. Ed has been fighting in the trenches for us tirelessly and is now building on Phyllis' legacy.

Ed's mettle was on display as we faced the head winds of "Billy Bush Weekend" going into the St. Louis debate, helping the campaign defend then-candidate Donald J. Trump on CNN day in and day out.

This book of *Trump Wins and Epic Speeches* is a continuation of that defense, and from that lessons on how to fight and win can be drawn.

What makes America great is people like Phyllis and Ed. And all of you reading this book.

Enjoy this list of Trump Wins and his Epic Speeches.

Let's never tire of winning!

Victory begets victory!

FIGHT ON EVERY DAY!

Stephen K. Bannon
Washington, D.C.
December 12, 2017

How to Use This Book

This book is a sword not a shield! It is a handbook of what President Trump has accomplished for you to use on other people. This reference guide includes not only the top Trump Wins of 2017 but also seven of his most definitive speeches of 2017. This is a book that you can hand to others and say "Face these facts" or "Get over your doubts and delusions." Buy as many copies as you can afford and mail them out like Christmas or birthday cards!

By listing 100 Trump Wins and especially by explaining the Top 40 Trump Wins (and their importance), I have armed you to spread the word about what the Trump administration has accomplished. For every Trump slam or snide comment, you will have more than a few Trump Wins with which to counter. Memorize a few, recall a few others, and deliver these goods with confidence.

This book also includes seven stirring Trump speeches sharing his vision, underlying governing philosophy, and view of Western Civilization. These words, loud and clear, echo his clarion call to "Make America Great Again" and will be recognized for years to come as a turning point in American history.

This book aims to break the spell of those who refuse to believe that Trump not only won the election but governs even today. These people deserve a thoughtful and considered effort to open their eyes.

This book is meant to invigorate all those who believe in President Trump. Give them a copy to fortify their defenses and get them on offense.

Finally, this book can sway some of those who remain on the fence, wondering if Trump truly is making, or even can make, America great again. Show them what he has done and what he is doing. They will get it and join the Trump train.

* * *

You will think that some Trump Wins are missing or not emphasized. Or that you disagree. That's your opinion and you are entitled to it. Hit me at ed@edmartinlive.com or at (314) 256-1776 with all comments and suggestions.

This book is more of a list than a research document. Acknowledgments and Sources are found at the end of the book and in an online catalogue that will be updated at EdMartinLive.com.

In putting together this book, I relied on thousands of folks many of whom I never met. Through email and social media, these folks gave me feedback on Trump Wins and how they saw things. Their support of the President is what is making his Presidency great!

Introduction

Donald Trump filled the doorway as Phyllis Schlafly and I looked up from our plastic seats. We needed one more chair in this tiny dressing room where I imagine showgirls did makeup and set their costumes. We were just a few feet off the stage of the Peabody Opera House in downtown St. Louis: me, Phyllis Schlafly and the next President of the United States of America.

It was early March 2016 and in a few moments Phyllis would endorse Mr. Trump before thousands of enthusiastic supporters who were already making noise on the other side of the dressing room wall.

The conversation between the three of us was driven by Phyllis.

"I spent decades making the Republican Party platform conservative," she said. "Pro-life, for military superiority, for the family, against big government and much more. And I need you to help me keep it conservative."

She handed him a copy of the 2012 Republican Party platform. Trump took it, opened it to a few pages, and said, "I know, and I'll do it. You can count on it."

But Phyllis wasn't done.

"One more thing" she said. "I need you to pick judges—at every level—like Scalia and Thomas. It's important."

Trump nodded and said, "I agree. I won't let you down on this. I promise."

* * *

President Trump has not let us down. At the Republican Convention in Cleveland, Trump's campaign adopted the most conservative platform in history. As President, Trump has cut funding to abortion, embraced military superiority and otherwise enacted conservative policies.

Even more importantly, he has especially delivered the promise he made to Phyllis with regard to judges. Starting with Neil Gorsuch on the Supreme Court, Trump's administration has methodically vetted, then nominated, well-qualified judges. The White House has carefully assisted the Senate in confirming these to the federal bench. This steadfast dedication to appointing Conservative members of the judiciary, in itself, will transform—and, more to the point, protect—America in the coming decades.

The media can scarcely believe all that Trump is accomplishing. In fact, rather than cover his impressive list of accomplishments, they have chosen to focus on such things as the President's golfing or his tweets. In doing so, they are missing a monumental presidency.

Trump's record speaks for itself. You may not like all that he has done or all that he is doing, but even a cursory review of his achievements, as cataloged by this book, shows that he is doing a lot. Moreover, the seven speeches included in this volume indicate Trump's depth of understanding of where we are in the world and where we are going.

For those of us who believe, it is clear we are making America great again! For those who disbelieve, I offer this book as an option for your future belief.

Top Trump Wins of 2017

Trump Win #1
Nominating Supreme Court Justice Neil Gorsuch

"When Justice Scalia passed away suddenly last February, I made a promise to the American people: If I were elected president, I would find the very best judge in the country for the Supreme Court. I promised to select someone who respects our laws and is representative of our Constitution and who loves our Constitution and someone who will interpret them as written. Today I am keeping another promise to the American people by nominating Judge Neil Gorsuch of the United States Supreme Court to be of the United States Supreme Court."

President Donald J. Trump, January 31, 2017

On January 31, 2017, Donald Trump kept his word by nominating the conservative Court of Appeals Judge Neil Gorsuch to fill the vacancy on the U.S. Supreme Court created by the untimely death of the late Justice Antonin Scalia. Gorsuch is a respected jurist with a long record of conservative judging. His opinions show respect for the Constitution and our Judeo-Christian values.

During the 2016 campaign, Donald Trump said repeatedly that he would nominate a "great conservative" to replace the late Justice Scalia. Donald Trump praised Scalia as a great judge, a fine man, and the kind of conservative America needs on the Supreme Court. Late in the campaign to show transparently the kind of men and women he would pick for the Scalia vacancy, Donald Trump released a list of twenty-one qualified judges from which he promised to pick. These twenty-one were widely regarded as high quality from top to bottom—it was created with the help of many of the more conservative leaders in America including Leonard Leo and Jonathan Bunch of the Federalist Society.

That Donald Trump stuck the nomination of the a quality conservative was only the start. After the nomination of Gorsuch, the management of his confirmation remains a credit to the President, his staff, and the Senate. It went smoothly and perfectly. Gorsuch was poised and smart in hearings. His opinions were thoughtful and respectful. He did draw a filibuster by the Democrats in the Senate but it was weak, pathetic and broken. Trump won, and so did we the people. For the next three or four decades, we can count on Justice Neil Gorsuch to serve as a conservative anchor on the United States Supreme Court. And, his nomination is a preview of the vacancy on the Supreme Court and how President Trump will handle it.

1

Trump Win #2
Transforming the Judiciary

"The judge story is an untold story; nobody wants to talk about it. But when you think about it, Mitch and I were saying, that has consequences 40 years out, depending on the age of the judge—but 40 years out."
President Donald J. Trump, October 2017

Senator Mitch McConnell's greatest gift to President Donald Trump and to the American people was his decision to stop confirming the federal judge nominees of President Barack Obama during the last months of Obama's presidency. This blockade stopped the replacement of Justice Antonin Scalia by an Obama liberal justice and it also kept dozens and dozens of other federal judgeships from being filled by Obama.

Trump has filled these many vacancies with conservatives who will serve for decades and will transform American law back to the constitution. Trump is—every week—nominating great conservatives who honor the law, respect the men and women in blue, and honor God. These nominees are being confirmed by a strong Republican majority in the Senate that doesn't care what the Democrats try to do.

During the week ending November 5, 2017, alone, the Senate confirmed four appeals judges along with one trial judge! These five join scores of other conservative lawyers who are nominated to fill the bench.

2

Trump Win #3
Melania & the First Family

"Donald is a wonderful husband, father and grandfather. He's strong, he's determined, bold and decisive. He's also compassionate, thoughtful, giving and loving."

Melania Trump, November 2016

Nothing the President Trump will do is as impressive as how his wife Melania put their son Barron first.

After his election in November 2016, President Trump and his wife made clear they would not move their son Barron to the White House right away. Why? Because Barron was in the middle of a school year. This made clear that family came first and is a model for all Americans.

What Mrs. Trump did at an event in Melbourne, Florida, on February 18, 2017, will stand out for its message of the centrality of faith in her life. Asked to introduce the President to the crowd, she began instead with the Lord's Prayer. Her heartfelt recitation of the prayer will echo in Americans' hearts for all time.

After her prayer, the President simply said, "Thank you, Melania."

Indeed, from all Americans, we say "Thank you and thank God" for the Trumps.

Trump Win #4
Staffing a Conservative Cabinet

"This is the most conservative cabinet of any Republican including Reagan"
American Conservative Union President Matt Schlapp

Donald Trump is a man who knows how to hire—and fire—great people. He campaigned on a promise to shake up things in Washington by positioning good leaders to serve with him—men and women dedicated to shrinking the size and scope of government and getting us back to the American basics outlined in the Constitution.

Health and Human Services Secretary Ben Carson has uncovered tens of millions of dollars of missing money while Education Secretary Betsy DeVos has limited government obstruction of education towards parents. Interior Secretary Ryan Zinke has moved to give back lands seized by the feds, and Attorney General Sessions is enforcing the law fearlessly against MS-13 and illegal aliens. Energy Secretary Rick Perry is getting his department back to basics—safety and science—instead of left-wing renewable energy schemes.

At the Defense Department, retired Marine Corps General James Mattis has reconfigured our military to be a fighting machine NOT a public relations vehicle for left-wing social engineering. At the State Department, Rex Tillerson has limited the bureaucrats and left scores of Obama positions unfilled that were more about politics than protecting or promoting American interests. United Nations Ambassador Nikki Haley has played a key role at pulling America away from foolish internationalist policies and toward protecting American interests. Commerce Secretary Wilbur Ross and Treasury Secretary Mnuchin are pushing deals for American companies and out of trade agreements that hurt us.

The Trump Cabinet puts Americans first by limiting the power of their departments (cutting regulations that were passed by the pen of Obama and his secretaries) and by making sure American interests are protected at home and abroad.

Trump Win #5
Growing the Economy to Record Heights

"(The) Numbers are phenomenal over the last (year)—since November 8th, Election Day. Our unemployment is at a 17-year low. We've gotten almost 2 million more people in the workforce in just that short period of time. I've reduced regulations terrifically, frankly, if I do say so myself."
President Donald J. Trump, November 6, 2017, Tokyo, Japan

Trump is right. The economy is soaring.

Donald Trump ran for President in large part to put Americans first by making the economy work for us not for the world and multinational corporations. He said he knew what to do. One year in, there is no disputing—even by the New York Times—that the economy is better today than it was the day he was in office.

The biggest part of this is that Donald Trump instills confidence in Americans that we can and will get be better. His confidence is contagious: it makes consumers and businesses and American people act. All indicators of consumer confidence are at records highs and the available indicators of economic strength are way up.

The proof is clear: Wall Street is setting record highs and creating wealth not just for big business but for all who own stocks and retirement accounts; GDP is up over 3% and soaring. This is real growth. Employment is down to the lowest it's been in almost a quarter of a century just over 4%. The Trump Tax Cut puts American taxpayers first and protects our American jobs by cutting American companies rates to levels lower than China—so our American companies can compete.

By year end, economists were arguing about whether the Trump economy can rev up to 6 or 7 percent in 2018. Truly, making the American economy great again!

Trump Win #6
Banning Lobbying by the Trump Administration

"We have begun to drain the swamp of government corruption by imposing a 5-year ban on lobbying by Executive Branch Officials, and a lifetime ban on becoming lobbyists for a foreign government."
President Donald J. Trump, January 28, 2017

Continuing on his pledge to "drain the Swamp," Donald Trump began his administration by immediately signing an executive order that bans Trump administration members from lobbying.

Signed on January 28, 2017, this executive order and later issued guidance includes the following provisions:
- A five-year ban from lobbying the agency in which they work
- A ban on lobbying ANY Trump administration
- A gift ban
- A ban on former Trump administration officials from ever lobbying for a foreign government

Although these may seem inconsequential when examined individually, as a whole they paint a vivid, broader picture of a President determined to not only drain the swamp but weed out its propensity to cultivate those who seek to gain and retain a lifetime of power, influence, and money for themselves at the taxpayer's expense.

Donald Trump ran for President without the need or aid of the big money lobbying class. He does not owe them anything - they do not own him like they own other politicians. This is unique in modern politics and makes draining the swamp possible.

Trump Win #7
Enacting the Travel Ban (& Extreme Vetting)

"Donald J. Trump is calling for a total and complete shutdown of Muslims entering the United States until our country's representatives can figure out what is going on."

Trump Campaign release on December 7, 2015

After three tries were all stymied by lower courts, President Trump's travel ban was finally upheld by the U.S. Supreme Court on December 4, 2017.

Throughout his presidential campaign, Donald Trump made clear that he would employ extreme vetting when it came to those trying to enter America. He has spent most of his first year directing all his executive agencies to use more extreme vetting and he has fought for travel bans on those visiting America who might be threats to our safety.

Almost immediately upon assuming office, President Trump issued a travel ban that blocked entry of people coming from certain nations without first having undergone extreme vetting. President Trump's executive order suspended the United States' refugee program for 120 days for travelers from six mostly Muslim countries and implemented a 90-day ban on travel to the United State from citizens of seven terror hot spots, including Iraq, Iran, Syria, Libya, Yemen. A partisan federal judge soon blocked the ban.

On March 7, the President issued another travel ban which, like its predecessor, was also blocked. President Trump has directed his Justice Department to fight all of these judicial rulings as wrong and dangerous to national security.

In the interim and before the December 4th ruling allowing him to proceed, President Trump continues to enforce travel restrictions under his executive branch authority by use of the existing laws and regulations. Late in the year, President Trump made clear to leaders in Europe that he recognized the threats that face us and them! Addressing Prime Minister Theresa May of Great Britain, President Trump wrote: "Theresa, don't focus on me, focus on the destructive Radical Islamic Terrorism that is taking place within the United Kingdom."

Trump Win #8
Pardoning Sheriff Joe Arpaio

"I am pleased to inform you that I have just granted a full Pardon to 85 year old American patriot Sheriff Joe Arpaio. He kept Arizona safe!"
                                        President Donald J. Trump, August 25, 2017

On Friday, August 25, 2017, President Donald Trump pardoned Sheriff Joe Arpaio of Arizona. Sheriff Arpaio had fought for the people of his state for decades and battled the federal government when it failed to enforce immigration laws.

Sheriff Joe always put Americans first. In doing so, he found himself vilified by the press. During a federal court case regarding the operation of his office, that of Sheriff of Maricopa County, Arpaio found himself held in contempt by a federal judge who simply did not like the sheriff's practices and policies, practices and policies it should be pointed out which remained wildly popular with Arpaio's constituents.

Sheriff Joe had disputed the findings, fearful that the liberal federal judge would not only hold him in contempt but perhaps even try to prosecute him.

In a move that echoed his ongoing theme of "Making America Great Again," Trump pardoned Sheriff Joe and praised him for his fearless leadership.

Arpaio responded by saying, "thank you for seeing my conviction for what it is: a political witch hunt by holdovers in the Obama justice department!'"

Trump Win #9
Draining the Swamp: Federal Hiring Freeze

"I'm generally not going to make a lot of appointments that would normally be made because you don't need them. I mean, you look at some of these agencies, how massive they are, and it's totally unnecessary. They have hundreds of thousands of people."
President Donald J. Trump, October 10, 2017

On January 23, 2017, President Trump signed a Presidential Memorandum directing a hiring freeze be implemented for all federal government agencies. The freeze was the culmination of a promise by candidate Donald Trump to slow the staggering growth of government and decrease the number of federal employees.

Even more importantly, President Trump has continued to not fill many senior positions which he believes to be unnecessary.

The growth in the number of federal employees has been astronomical over the past decades. By stopping the hiring and slowing the growth, Trump is saving money and limiting government. Another benefit rests in the fact that the first step in draining any swamp is preventing it from filling up even more.

Trump Win #10
Isolating "Little Rocket Man" & North Korea

"We got to close it down, because he's getting too close to doing something ... Right now, he's probably got the weapons, but he doesn't have the transportation system. Once he has the transportation system, he's sick enough to use it. So we better get involved."

Candidate Donald J. Trump, January 6, 2016

Like his father before him, Kim Jong Un of North Korea has antagonized U.S. presidents for more than a decade. Now, though, it seems he has met his match in Donald J. Trump. President Trump nicknamed Kim Jong Un the "little rocket man" and mocked his failures in the missile and nuclear program.

Unlike his predecessors, President Trump has made clear that America will not be put into an insecure position and North Korea will be stopped. He has gone about isolating North Korea economically and politically.

In November, President Trump visited Asia and received support from a variety of Asian nations, including China, in his efforts to further isolate the Hermit Kingdom.

On November 7, 2017, President Trump delivered a powerful address before the South Korean National Assembly. There, he made clear that North Korea should not "try us" while reminding the world that we want peace through strength.

Under the tyrannical rule of Kim Jong Un, North Korea is being out-maneuvered and hemmed in by the strength and resolve exhibited by President Trump. The President has made clear we are at war—an economic war—with North Korea. The result is that the nation of North Korea will be crippled until its tyrannical leader stops his aggression toward the world at large.

Trump Win #11
Killing ISIS

"We are going to convene my top generals and give them a simple instruction. They will have 30 days to submit to the Oval Office a plan for soundly and quickly defeating ISIS. We have no choice."
Candidate Donald J. Trump, September 6, 2016

During his first days as President, Donald J. Trump asked for his military to develop a plan to destroy ISIS and kill its fighters. He did not hold a press conference to announce his intention to "lead from behind" or revealing when he intended to invade a major city. Those days and that administration were gone.

Instead, President Trump demanded and received a thoughtful and thorough plan which he then asked his leaders to execute. President Trump hired General James Mattis, the "warrior monk," to lead the Department of Defense in killing ISIS. No shrinking violet, "Mad Dog" Mattis made it clear from the outset his intention to hurt the enemy at all turns.

So steadfast is the General's resolve that when asked on Face the Nation what keeps him awake at night, General Mattis offered this chilling and direct reply: "Nothing. I keep other people awake at night."

If there had been any doubt that America was back in the business of eliminating bad players on the world stage, those words put to rest that notion. As a result of America's renewed interest in winning the War on Terror, neither ISIS or other groups spend as much time on social media bragging about their "successes." Moreover, Mattis and our military have marched ISIS back out of Raqqa.

With the help of patriots like General James Mattis, President Donald J. Trump is ruthlessly pursuing the destruction of ISIS. As a result, the Land of the Free and the Home of the Brave has learned to sleep just a bit easier each night.

Trump Win #12
Winning Twitter

"My use of social media is not Presidential—it's MODERN DAY PRESIDENTIAL."

@realDonaldTrump, July 1, 2017

President Donald J. Trump has single-handedly transformed American political life through his use of social media, specifically Twitter.

He has become the most accessible political leader in human history by responding to the American people's interests and objections via his Twitter account.

For example, when the Trump administration announced that it would allow certain elephant hunting changes, many Americans took to social media to protest. After a few days of thoughtful consideration, President Trump announced in a tweet that he had heard the concerns and would look into them. He soon suspended the changes.

Utilizing the power of Twitter, President Trump also directs the media to cover the issues he believes are important. This stands in stark contrast to years of antagonistic press members goading those with whom they disagree (almost always Republican) and guiding the narrative to suit their desires.

If you follow him on Twitter, you will learn about the Constitution and how a President is limited in his role. Contrary to what the left, and by extension a sympathetic press, will have the public believe, Trump is no dictator but an executive who must work within the three branches of government.

President Trump does not limit his tweets to political points or gamesmanship, he also has fun with them. Through his account, he encourages people in their lives and in their work. Much to their continued consternation, every time critics demand that President Trump stop using Twitter, it seems he redoubles his tweeting ... to the delight of his supporters everywhere.

Trump Win #13
Taking on Fake News

"Congratulations to ABC News for suspending Brian Ross for his horrendously inaccurate and dishonest report on the Russia, Russia, Russia Witch Hunt. More Networks and 'papers' should do the same with their Fake News!"

President Donald J. Trump, December 3, 2017

One of the hallmarks of both candidate and President Donald J. Trump has been his enthusiastic willingness to call out the mainstream media for misleading and provocative practices within the powerful medium. By labeling certain elements within the media "fake news," President Trump has driven home the point that many in the media not only harbor a political viewpoint but that they are often, if not always, abusing their position to make those points, however covertly or overtly.

In particular, President Trump has focused his attention on media "leaders" like the The Washington Post, owned and funded by Jeff Bezos, billionaire owner of Amazon. Bezos is not a disinterested party in Washington, D.C. and has attacked President Trump's administration in many ways. Under Bezos' direction, The Washington Post seems especially resistant in the President's efforts to drain the swamp and defend American sovereignty by stopping illegal immigration.

Time and again, President Trump has made it clear that the era of yellow journalism is not a part of our past but, rather, a clear and present danger to our democratic process and the reputation of honest and fair journalists everywhere.

Trump Win #14
No More Tax Dollars for International Abortion

"We applaud President Trump's action today to restore the Mexico City Policy, which withholds taxpayer funds from foreign non-governmental organizations that promote or perform abortions overseas (often in violation of the host country's own laws). This is a welcome step toward restoring and enforcing important federal policies that respect the most fundamental human right—the right to life—as well as the long-standing, bipartisan consensus against forcing Americans to participate in the violent act of abortion."
Cardinal Timothy Dolan, Chairman of the Catholic Bishops Pro-Life Committee, January 23, 2017

On January 23, 2017, President Trump stopped American tax dollars from being spent on abortion in overseas organizations and countries by signing a memorandum reinstating the Mexico City policy.

The Mexico City Policy directs the Secretary of State and the administrator of the USAID, as well as other government entities, to follow a January 2001 Presidential Memorandum which blocked our tax dollars from being spent on abortion.

President Obama had rescinded the Mexico City Policy and subsequently U.S. tax dollars once again began funding overseas organizations that supported abortion.

President Trump campaigned as a pro-lifer and promised to stop tax dollars from going to abortion and abortion providers. He has delivered but waits on Congress to help him defund Planned Parenthood.

Trump Win #15
Forcing Weakling RINOs to Quit

"Great to see that Dr. Kelli Ward is running against Flake Jeff Flake, who is WEAK on borders, crime and a non-factor in Senate. He's toxic!"
President Donald J. Trump August 17, 2017

In October, Senator Jeff Flake of Arizona announced that he would not be seeking re-election, admitting that "he couldn't win the primary as a Republican" because Trump has moved the party toward America first policies.

Donald Trump has helped America win bits of her heart and soul back by getting people like Senator Jeff Flake and Senator Bob Corker (to name just a few) to abandon runs for reelection and, in the process, abandon efforts to forestall putting America first. They oppose Trump on many policies and support liberal policies like amnesty for illegals and trade deals that hurt America. Flake and Corker are establishment politicians who support the failed globalist policies of the past. Well, they used to. Soon enough, their efforts will be mere footnotes in history.

Congressman Charlie Dent of Pennsylvania is another Never-Trump type, pro-abortion and liberal on far too many issues. He, too, quit rather than run for re-election.

Slowly but surely, Trump is draining the swamp of not only practices which hurt the American people but those that support or advocate those policies as well.

Trump Win #16
Bombing Syria: Message of Peace Through Strength

"It is in this vital national security interest of the United States to prevent and deter the spread and use of deadly chemical weapons. There can be no dispute that Syria used banned chemical weapons, violated its obligations under the Chemical Weapons Convention and ignored the urging of the U.N. Security Council."

President Donald J. Trump, April 7, 2017

In early April, Syria gassed and killed over 80 of its citizens. This heinous act became even more despicable when photographs revealed that children were among the victims. The world wondered how Donald Trump, just over two months after being inaugurated, would respond.

His words reflected the feeling of many worldwide.

"When you kill innocent children, innocent babies—babies, little babies—with a chemical gas that is so lethal—people were shocked to hear what gas it was—that crosses many, many lines, beyond a red line. Many, many lines."

He reminded the press and the world of a philosophy he had stated and restated many times during the campaign.

"One of the things I think you've noticed about me is militarily I don't like to say where I'm going and what I'm doing. I'm not saying I'm doing anything one way or the other. But I'm certainly not going to be telling you."

Next, though, came what would eventually be recognized as a warning that neither he nor the United States under his watch would stand for such atrocities. On April 6, President Trump launched 59 Tomahawk missiles and destroyed a Syrian government airfield, making certain first that civilians and others nearby understood what was happening in order to minimize deaths.

The President had answered the question of just how he would respond to such actions by making a calculated, careful, and forceful strike, in the process reminding the world that strong and decisive leadership would once again win the day.

Trump Win #17
Putting America First on Trade

"The Trans-Pacific Partnership is another disaster done and pushed by special interests who want to rape our country—just a continuing rape of our country ... It's a harsh word, but it's true."
Candidate Donald J. Trump, June 28, 2016

January 23, just three days into his nascent presidency, Donald Trump made good on his promise to pull out of the Trans-Pacific Partnership by signing an executive action ending our participation.

Since that time, the President has directed his administration to stop the implementation of NAFTA and to prompt both Canada and Mexico to renegotiate in an effort to not only make things work better but to be more equitable to the United States in the process. Additionally, he appointed staffers and leadership, including Peter Navarro, to positions in the administration to limit the damage done by the free-trade deals and look for opportunities to roll them back.

While visiting China in November, President Trump made it clear that he did not blame China for taking advantage of America. After all, as a businessman, he recognized that good business means getting the best possible deal. Rather, he blamed previous administrations for allowing themselves to be taken advantage of and making lopsided deals that favored everyone but the United States.

He has also raised the tariffs on some goods, such as lumber from Canada as well as others, in order to bring some balance back to our trade efforts. President Trump has made clear that if we have to add more tariffs we will because this leads to American jobs.

Of all his wins, perhaps this has most resonated with the American people because it directly impacted them by adding more and more jobs.

Trump Win #18
Fighting the Opioid Crisis, Personally

"No part of our society—not young or old, rich or poor, urban or rural—has been spared this plague of drug addiction and this horrible, horrible situation that's taken place with opioids. This epidemic is a national health emergency."

President Donald J. Trump, October 26, 2017

On October 26, President Trump declared the opioid crisis to be a public health emergency. This declaration allows the federal government to act vigorously and quickly within its various agencies to stop the drug that claimed more than 59,000 lives in 2016 alone.

Trump made it clear that he was acting this way because he recognized that this crisis affected every aspect of our country from crime to health and wellbeing and beyond. It truly is a national crisis.

The President remarked, "No part of our society—not young or old, rich or poor, urban or rural—has been spared this plague of drug addiction and this horrible, horrible situation that's taken place with opioids. This epidemic is a national health emergency."

In describing the impact of addiction, Donald Trump spoke movingly about his own brother, Fred, who had died from alcohol addiction.

Once again, President Trump had proven to be a man, not above the people, but of the people. He not only understood their cares, concerns, and tragedies, he shared them. Now he would lead them in helping to eradicate one of the most dangerous poisons to our culture—opioid addiction.

Trump Win #19
Greatest Tax Cut in History & Obamacare Repealed

"I promised the American people a big, beautiful tax cut for Christmas.
With final passage of this legislation, that is exactly what they are getting."
President Donald J. Trump, December 20, 2017

On Wednesday, December 20th, President Donald Trump signed the historic Tax Cut and Jobs Act (Trump Tax Cut). The Trump Tax Cut reduced the tax burden for almost all Americans who pay taxes by $1.5 trillion.

The Trump Tax Cut also made our American businesses more competitive by cutting corporate rates below China's rates. (We will now pay 21% while China charges 25%!) Corporations estimate that more than $4 trillion will return to America due to the Trump Tax Cut.

There are increased tax deductions for families and children. For example, the tax credit for a dependent child is doubled to $2,000. It also treats certain expenses for private schools (or, in some cases, homeschooling) favorably. The Trump Tax Cut decreases the Estate Tax dramatically so that families can leave their wealth to their children without paying taxes on that wealth a second time (leaving it in place for only the wealthiest Americans).

Importantly, the Trump Tax Cut effectively repealed Obamacare by eliminating the individual mandate that required Americans to purchase insurance or pay a penalty. The Trump Tax Cut reduced the tax penalty in Obamacare to zero thus ending it. By gutting the government control of healthcare purchasing, President Trump is freeing up the market to deliver more choices and lower costs.

Trump Win #20
Saying "Merry Christmas" not "Happy Holidays"

"Today's a day that I've been looking very much forward to all year long. And now, as the president of the United States, it's my tremendous honor to finally wish America and the world a very merry Christmas."
President Donald J. Trump at the 2017 White House Christmas Tree Lighting

"We're Saying Merry Christmas again."
Candidate Donald J. Trump

President Donald Trump campaigned for president on a platform that included embracing political incorrectness and returning the nation to the American values so long identified with our country. One way he made this clear was in his promise that he would lead Americans in saying "Merry Christmas" once again.

At the Values Voter Summit in Washington, D.C. in the fall, President Trump fired up the crowd by reminding them of this promise. Just weeks later at the 2017 White House Christmas Tree Lighting, he delivered on that promise. His short speech, found at http://bit.ly/TrumpWin20, is powerful.

President Trump's focus on Christmas is not simply related to the holiday. Rather, it signals a return to America's roots. In his Poland speech, Trump spoke of defending Western civilization, including placing our collective confidence in faith traditions such as Christianity.

In a sign of true diversity and inclusion, President Trump also allowed the celebration of Jewish holy days at the White House, an obvious nod to his Jewish daughter, son-in-law, and grandchildren. President Trump said, "At Christmas we are reminded more than ever that the family is the bedrock of American life."

Trump went on to end the celebration of Muslim holidays at the White House, and Judeo-Christian traditions are once more being honored, just as they had been throughout our history—a history sadly aborted in January of 2009.

Christmas wins because of this President!

Trump Win #21
Fighting Illegal Immigration

"Build that wall!"

Chant at virtually every Trump campaign rally

Donald Trump directed his administration to begin building a wall on the southern border of our country.

True to form as a businessman, he asked that prototypes be built to review specs, structure, and viability.

One of those prototypes, presented in October of this year, is not only under review by the Trump Administration but looks to be the design which will serve as the basis for the wall.

As before, Trump reiterated his preference that the wall have some see-through aspects, meaning that the structure will not only stop intruding illegal aliens but allowing good neighbors to see one other.

From the moment he descended the escalator in Trump Tower and declared his candidacy, Trump has remained committed to building not just a wall on the southern border but, rather, "The Wall" his supporters repeatedly cried out for.

21

Trump Win #22
Helping Persecuted Christians in the Middle East

*"Across the wider Middle East, we can now see a future in many areas
without a Christian faith. But tonight, I came to tell you: Help is on the way
.... [We will take] the fight to terrorists on our terms, on their soil. We will
not rest, we will not relent, until we hunt down and destroy ISIS at its source,
so it can no longer threaten our people or anyone who calls the Middle East
home."*

Vice President Mike Pence, October 26, 2017

Many Americans have watched with concern as the persecution of
Christians has increased throughout the world and especially in the Middle
East. President Obama and his administration seemed unconcerned and relied
on the ineffective United Nations to address the concerns.

President Trump changed course. He is unafraid to address the concerns
and make them an issue. He has repeatedly called for freedom for imprisoned
Christian pastors including Evangelical Pastor Andrew Brunson who is jailed
in Turkey. President Trump assigned the problem to Vice President Mike
Pence. Pence has put public attention on the issue through speeches and
visits. He has also addressed the problem of the United Nations. Pence said
that we will be "stopping the ineffective relief efforts at the United Nations
and from this day forward making sure America will provide support directly
to the persecuted communities through our administration."

Over the past decade, during wars in the Middle East, the Islamic
extremists have targeted Christians by beheading them and torturing them.
President Trump has been unafraid to address Christian persecution and fight
its perpetrators. Through this and by fighting ISIS and Islamic terrorism,
President Trump is protecting all Americans and stopping persecution of
Christians.

Trump Win #23
Getting 1.5 Million People Off Food Stamps

"President Obama has almost doubled our national debt to more than $19 trillion, and growing. Yet what do we have to show for it? Our roads and bridges are falling apart, our airports are in third-world condition, and 43 million Americans are on food stamps."

Candidate Donald J. Trump, July 21, 2016

President Obama made a priority of growing both the size and scope of government programs, including food stamps, disability, and other programs. This led to often-unchecked corruption including "gaming the system."

Unlike Obama, however, the Trump economy has created jobs which indirectly addressed such fraud by causing a total number of almost 1.5 million people to no longer require such assistance. This 3.5% drop in the number of people receiving food stamps began immediately after Trump assumed office and has steadily continued.

So much so, that Trump's 2018 budget proposal cuts the food stamp program back even further because he knows that it will be less and less necessary.

Additionally, Trump has instituted a work requirement for able-bodied adults before they may be considered eligible to receive food stamps. Obama would never have dreamed of asking citizens to take such responsibility for themselves.

It seems only fair: If someone is going to get help in the form of food stamps, then he should at least exhibit some sign that he is trying to provide for himself. What better way than looking for gainful employment?

Trump Win #24
Managing Back-to-Back Hurricanes

"Trump's response to hurricane was perfect"
CNN.com Headline, September 5, 2017

An unprecedented hurricane season struck the United States and nearby nations, with Texas, Florida, Puerto Rico, and other parts of the Caribbean being particularly hard hit.

Trump handled the hurricane emergencies like no president before him: not Bill Clinton during Hurricane Andrew; not George W. Bush amid the destruction of Hurricane Katrina; and not even media darling Obama during Hurricane Sandy and the Joplin tornadoes.

Like others, he visited the scenes of devastation and comforted those who were hurt and devastated. Even his critics agreed that he managed the government and the crisis incredibly well.

However, when it appeared that the hurricane aid which was so desperately needed in the region of Texas would be threatened by bipartisan inaction, Trump struck a deal with Democrats to forge and pass a clean bill ensuring that the hurricane funds could, and would, be allocated immediately.

In a time of crisis Trump stepped up, and America and the world saw his leadership.

Trump Win #25
No to Paris; Yes to Pittsburgh

"I was elected to represent the citizens of Pittsburgh, not Paris. I promised I would exit or renegotiate any deal which fails to serve America's interests."
President Donald J. Trump, June 1, 2017

With this simple, yet profound, statement Donald Trump pulled America out of the Paris Accord, a business-crippling international agreement, the brunt of which America looked to assume. Trump stated clearly, "The Paris accord will undermine (our) economy," and "puts (us) at a permanent disadvantage."

President Trump recognized what average Americans seemed to instinctively understand—that the Paris Accord had proven to be yet another international organization funded by American tax dollars and fueled by a future that foreigners would administer. The Paris Accord required American taxpayers to give billions of dollars to the Paris Accord bureaucrats and to change our economy. Meanwhile, other nations—including China—did not have to pay as much nor change their behavior. (In addition, China and others showed a willingness to ignore any rules they were required to obey— they would say yes to the deal but ignore the requirements. See, for example, China on trade and the WTO.)

America has its own problems and issues with which we must contend, and the disproportionate payment by America to the Paris Accord and its attendant organizers were an outrage too far for a President who had pledged to put, and keep, America first.

Trump Win #26
Taking on the UN

"With this anti-Israel bias that's long documented on the part of UNESCO, that needs to come to an end."
State Department Spokeswoman Heather Nauert, October 12, 2017

President Trump took the first steps toward pulling America out of UNESCO, a United Nations (UN) boondoggle allowing international organizations to take American monies with which they then fund educational efforts that are decidedly anti-American and apathetic to both our culture and founding principles.

Since assuming her post, President Trump's Ambassador to the United Nations, Nikki Haley, has proven time and again to be a fearless defender of American interests within the UN. She has called for reforms where needed and continued to press UN leadership when they seemed to lack either the spirit or the spine to act.

Many Americans wish President Trump would pull out of the UN completely, but Ambassador Hailey stands as a good indicator that it is no longer "business as usual" at the United Nations.

Trump Win #27
Releasing the JFK Documents

"JFK Files are being carefully released. In the end there will be great transparency. It is my hope to get just about everything to public!"
@realDonaldTrump, October 27, 2017

In October, Donald Trump directed the release of all documents related to President John F. Kennedy's assassination, all of which had been kept sealed for a quarter of a century under a Congressional law.

Although Trump wanted to release all the documents, at the last minute a number of them were held back by both the CIA and the FBI. The President directed these agencies to review the documents they were holding back and then release them quickly. A second release followed shortly thereafter.

At the time of this publishing. almost all of the JFK documents have been released.

Their importance cannot be overstated as they reveal important facts vital to our national security, even today, such as the fact that anti-American forces met in Cuba, Mexico, and in the United States.

The documents also reveal that the treachery of the deep state existed even then.

Though the release may not have answered all of the questions surrounding the JFK assassination, the move honored the principle that a government should be transparent to its people.

Trump Win #28
Stand for the Flag and the National Anthem

"Very important that NFL players STAND tomorrow, and always, for the playing of our National Anthem. Respect our Flag and our Country!"
                                    @realDonaldTrump, September 30, 2017

Donald Trump said what most Americans felt: Millionaire football players have no business kneeling during the national anthem or the Pledge of Allegiance.

While many politicians pushed back on Trump's aggressive stance in favor of the flag and the national anthem, the American people remained squarely on his side. Secure in this knowledge, the President doubled, tripled, and quadrupled down on his stance by repeatedly reminding the league, the commissioner, and the owners that he thought such actions deserved punishment—including being fired.

The Commissioner of the National Football League, Roger Goodell, made a terrible, tactical mistake in allowing his players to disrespect the anthem and the flag as they did. Even he seemed to recognize this as the protests wore on and his own position seemed to waver depending upon his audience.

Trump never yielded.

Ultimately, the NFL players once again began standing during the anthem, although they found other ways to make points about policy and their now-proven skewed priorities.

Trump Win #29
Hiring Stephen Miller & Stephen Bannon

"I want to thank Steve Bannon for his service. He came to the campaign during my run against Crooked Hillary Clinton—it was great!"
                                    @realDonaldTrump, August 19, 2017

"Congratulations Stephen Miller—on representing me this morning on the various Sunday morning shows. Great job!"
                                    @realDonaldTrump, February 12, 2017

Every presidential administration sees the rise of certain players who will serve a big role in governing. Karl Rove and David Axelrod are just a few examples of such power players.

Donald Trump and his presidency took two men and put them at the pinnacle of American thought and leadership.

One is Steve Bannon, whose fearless promotion of economic nationalism and power to the people is now clear to the world. His success in the White House—his famous white boards of tasks to accomplish is now clearer than ever. And his defense of western civilization and American exceptionalism will go on for decades. This is all to Trump's credit.

Stephen Miller, a thirty-something policy aid and speech writer, deftly crafts the words and weaves the policies into Trump's speeches. Miller is a disciple of Larry Elder and David Horowitz and trained in the office of Senator Jeff Sessions. Miller is by far the most influential speech writer and policy aide of the modern era.

Trump Win #30
Signing an Executive Order for Religious Freedom

"[N]o American should be forced to choose between the dictates of the federal government and the tenets of their faith."
                                        President Donald J. Trump, May 5, 2017

On the campaign trail, Donald Trump stated that a priority would be to preserve and protect the religious liberty of all Americans, not just those with a stamp of approval from the left.

His religious order from May 2017 focused on four primary points. First, it included broad language to vigorously enforce religious freedom protection.

Second, this order instructed IRS officials to protect the freedom of churches and houses of worship.

Third, the order directs federal officials, including HHS, to consider issuing amended regulations for nonprofits and faith-based groups to protect against abortion conscience.

Fourth, and finally, the order adopts the Attorney General's guidance interpreting the religious liberty protections and federal law as allowing anyone to opt out based on their conscience. This effectively gutted the Johnson Amendment (which was sought in the tax bill proposals more formally).

Best of all, Trump stated that protections within the law will allow anyone to object to Obamacare provisions that required coverage of contraception and abortions.

Trump Win #31
NATO Spending Up; NATO Allies Stepping Up

"This is not fair to the people and taxpayers of the United States, and many of these nations owe massive amounts of money from past years and [from] not paying in those past years."
President Donald J. Trump, May 25, 2017 to NATO Leaders in Brussels

On May 25, Present Trump met with North Atlantic Treaty Organization (NATO) leaders in Brussels and proceeded to identify what he considered to be a major problem with their conduct. The NATO allies had not been, in his estimation, "paying what they should be paying."

Our NATO allies are supposed to spend a certain amount on their own defenses and not simply rely on the Americans to pay this tab.

Within weeks of this criticism, NATO allies announced that they would increase defense spending by as much as 4.3% this year. The Secretary General of NATO, Jens Stoltenberg, proclaimed this as a clear demonstration that our alliance stands united in the face of any possible aggression.

This stands in stark contrast to the previous eight years of bowing and conceding, essentially leaving America to fend for itself in matters large and small. There is a new sheriff in town, and he is not inclined to bow.

Ed Martin

Trump Win #32
Improving Healthcare for Veterans

"For many years, the government failed to keep its promises to our veterans. We all remember the nightmare that veterans suffered during the VA scandals that were exposed a few years ago."

President Donald J. Trump, June 23, 2017

In June, President Trump signed the Accountability and Whistleblower Protection Act of 2017. This law, passed by Congress, empowered the Secretary of Veterans Affairs to discipline and fire employees for misconduct within the Veterans' Administration.

On the campaign trail, Trump had promised to improve VA health care and this law addressed the most egregious aspect of VA mismanagement: the fact that employees could not be disciplined or made to toe the line.

President Trump's VA Secretary, Dr. David Shaw, praised the act as a way to improve both morale within the rank and file as well as the care for those to whom we as a nation owe so much.

While the media and others prefer to cover perceived slights and fabricated conspiracies, laws like these are not only making government work better, they are improving the quality of life for millions of our fellow citizens.

Trump Win #33
Ending Obama's Transgender Military Experiments

"After consultation with my Generals and military experts, please be advised that the United States Government will not accept or allow transgender individuals to serve in any capacity in the U.S. Military. Our military must be focused on decisive and overwhelming victory and cannot be burdened with the tremendous medical costs and disruption that transgender in the military would entail. Thank you."

@realDonaldTrump, July 26, 2017

In July, President Trump announced that he would stop the social engineering and experimentation in the military that Obama pushed through by executive order in January just before leaving office.

Trump clearly stated that he would stop the transgender service members from serving openly and enlisting. Trump stated the transgender people should not be recruited and shouldn't serve in the military because of the distractions and costs. Trump's vision of our military is that it is a fighting force that must be focused on military superiority and not a social agency for experimentation.

In August, Trump formalized his policy with an executive order. As expected, this was challenged in court and, unfortunately, an activist judge, Judge Colleen Kollar-Kotelly of the Federal District Court for the District of Columbia, issued an injunction blocking Trump's policy.

Yet again this sets up the constitutional conflict between the commander-in-chief and the judiciary. This is a fight that Americans should want resolved in favor of the Constitution against judicial overreach.

Trump Win #34
Firing the Compromised James Comey

"Comey lost the confidence of almost everyone in Washington, Republican and Democrat alike. When things calm down, they will be thanking me!"
President Donald J. Trump, May 10, 2017

On May 9, Donald Trump fired Federal Bureau of Investigation (FBI) Director James Comey for incompetence and proving to be a political actor beyond the scope of his job.

Comey has now been shown to have actively mismanaged the investigation of Hillary Clinton's emails as well as having been party to the unmasking of documents by the Obama administration during its waning days. Even a cursory glance at his record proves Comey to have been both compromised and ineffective in his job.

Trump fired Comey, a subordinate member of the executive branch of which Donald Trump remains both the titular and actual leader. This inconvenient, Constitutional fact seems to have largely boggled or bypassed the media which decried the move as partisan.

That Trump had the courage to stand up and honor his Constitutional commitment stands as a credit to his office and his sense of self.

Trump Win #35
Dropping the Mother of All Bombs (MOAB)

Acting on what President Trump called his "total authorization," the United States armed forces on Thursday dropped a GBU 43/B device onto a maze of tunnels and bunkers occupied by ISIS terrorists in eastern Afghanistan's Nangahar Province. This Massive Ordnance Air Blast weapon affectionately is nicknamed the Mother of All Bombs (MOAB). America's most powerful non-atomic armament blasted these catacombs of hate with the equivalent of eleven tons of TNT.

Deroy Murdock, April 18, 2017, *National Review*

On April 13, Donald Trump directed that the mother of all bombs be dropped in Afghanistan, close to the Pakistan border. Although the official name of the weapon stands as GBU-43/B massive ordnance air blast bomb, most enlisted personnel and their superiors recognize the weapon by its nickname—the MOAB.

Once the MOAB had been deployed, 36 ISIS fighters had been neutralized and served no further danger to us or our way of life.

When asked about the bombing, Trump said, "Everybody knows exactly what happened. What I do is authorize my military. We have the greatest military in the world and they have done the job as usual."

Originally built in 2003 at a weight of 21,500 pounds, the MOAB has a blast radius of one mile in all directions and contains the equivalent of 11 tons of TNT.

Trumps' willingness to utilize the MOAB and all of its destructive power sent a clear message to both enemies and allies alike. The sleeping giant that is the United States had been awakened after an eight-year slumber.

Trump Win #36
Creating More Than 1 Million Jobs

"Excellent Jobs Numbers just released—and I have only just begun. Many job stifling regulations continue to fall. Movement back to USA!"

@realDonaldTrump, August 4, 2017

Candidate Donald Trump ran for President promising that job creation would be a top priority. During each month of his first year in office, President Donald Trump has more than lived up to his pledge.

A little less than eight months into his presidency, in August, Trump's economy had created more than one million jobs. By year's end, it that number had nearly doubled to two million!

How did he do this? President Trump took two specific actions.

First, he made certain that his optimism and energy were apparent, each and every time he spoke about the future of the American economy. So palpable was his feeling of hope that the American people found themselves caught up in this renewed wellspring of America-can-do, as evidenced by surging consumer confidence.

Second, President Trump cut economy-killing regulations, especially those Obama suspiciously rushed to implement during his administration's final days.

As most economists consider job creation to be a more accurate gauge of an economy's basic health than the easily manipulated unemployment numbers, it remains apparent that the general economic surge and rapid growth of job creation under Trump has proven time and again to be a promise kept.

Trump Win #37
No Amnesty for Obama's Dreamers

"Similarly, no cabinet secretary has the power, through guidance, letters or otherwise, to wipe entire sections of immigration law. But that's what the previous administration did with its Deferred Action for Childhood Arrivals, or DACA, policy ... Once again, the Department advised and the administration put an end to it—and it is being ended now."
Attorney General Jeff Sessions, November 2017

Barack Obama created DACA in 2012, as he had so many times before in other areas, via executive order. This order, though, proved to be both insidious and potentially crippling to our country as it served as a means by which illegal aliens, brought into America at a young age, would be given amnesty and a path to citizenship. It's unconstitutionality seemed undeniable as it bypassed Congress in re-writing immigration laws.

Donald Trump campaigned on a promise to end DACA, and in October he announced that the program would end in six months for those who are enrolled in the program.

More than 800,000 people were already enrolled with over one million others eligible. By shutting down this program, Trump blocked amnesty for these people living in violation of the law.

Trump Win #38
No Amnesty for Dreamers' Parents

"In the case of DAPA ... that was immediately enjoined by the courts and it languished in limbo for now I think two or three years, so my action was just to do a little house cleaning and I canceled the memo."

Secretary John Kelly

In June, President Trump's then Department of Homeland Security Secretary, John Kelly, signed a memorandum rescinding Obama's effort to grant amnesty to illegal immigrants' parents.

The Deferred Action for Parents of Americans (DAPA) fools virtually no one as it remains a euphemism for "amnesty," allowing approximately four million illegals into America. Obama both dreamed up this program up and breathed life into it via his pen—"executive order"—without Congressional approval. This proved to be just another in a series of moves by Obama to use his executive power in aiding and abetting illegal aliens.

Individuals and states alike challenged DAPA leading to the federal courts blocking the program as improper. However, these court decisions remained pending and eligible for appeal.

By ordering the rescinding of DAPA by his Homeland Security Department, Trump ended all chance for appeal and foreclosed amnesty for these millions.

Trump Win #39
Targeting MS-13 Gangs & Supporting Police

"I am announcing that I have authorized them to use every lawful tool to investigate MS-13—not just our drug laws, but everything from RICO to our tax laws to our firearms laws."

Attorney General Jeff Session, October 2017

In a speech to law enforcement officers in Long Island in late July, President Trump committed again to fighting the criminals and standing with our men and women in blue. He has followed through by instructing General Sessions to fight the war on MS-13 and for ICE officials to enforce all laws.

The American people know that MS-13 is a vicious gang with ties to Latin America. It is the scourge of major cities and relies heavily on illegal immigrants to commit crimes of violence and drug dealing. What we needed was a President willing to fight.

President Trump has called these gang members "animals" who have "transformed peaceful parks and beautiful, quiet neighborhoods into bloodstained killing fields." He has vowed that we will destroy MS-13.

Finally, President Trump has unfailingly supported our men and women in blue. He recognizes their sacrifice and gives them the tools to do their jobs.

Trump Win #40
Cutting Regulations: 2-for-1

"The American dream is back ... This isn't a knock (only) on President Obama; this is a knock on many presidents preceding me ... Regulation has been horrible for big business, but it's been worse for small business."

President Donald J. Trump, January 2017

On Monday, January 30th, President Trump signed an executive order aimed at drastically cutting regulations. His order directs that no regulation may be created without first removing two regulations. Also, the cost of all regulations must be clearly identified by his Cabinet Secretaries before implementation.

By October, the President could safely say that "(w)e've cut more regulations than any president in history—by far, it's not even a contest" and have it confirmed by fact-checking by liberal media! He has cut regulations, withdrawn recently filed rules, and cut red-tape.

Many liberal pundits wonder why the Trump economy is soaring but more and more leading economists agree that the Trump administration's regulatory system is key to the success.

Epic
Trump Speeches
of 2017

Inaugural Address
January 20, 2017
West Side of the U.S. Capitol

Chief Justice Roberts, President Carter, President Clinton, President Bush, President Obama, fellow Americans, and people of the world: thank you.

We, the citizens of America, are now joined in a great national effort to rebuild our country and to restore its promise for all of our people.

Together, we will determine the course of America and the world for years to come.

We will face challenges. We will confront hardships. But we will get the job done.

Every four years, we gather on these steps to carry out the orderly and peaceful transfer of power, and we are grateful to President Obama and First Lady Michelle Obama for their gracious aid throughout this transition. They have been magnificent.

Today's ceremony, however, has very special meaning. Because today we are not merely transferring power from one Administration to another, or from one party to another – but we are transferring power from Washington, D.C. and giving it back to you, the American People.

For too long, a small group in our nation's Capital has reaped the rewards of government while the people have borne the cost.

Washington flourished–but the people did not share in its wealth.

Politicians prospered–but the jobs left, and the factories closed.

The establishment protected itself, but not the citizens of our country.

Their victories have not been your victories; their triumphs have not been your triumphs; and while they celebrated in our nation's Capital, there was little to celebrate for struggling families all across our land.

That all changes–starting right here, and right now, because this moment is your moment: it belongs to you.

It belongs to everyone gathered here today and everyone watching all across America.

This is your day. This is your celebration.

And this, the United States of America, is your country.

What truly matters is not which party controls our government, but whether our government is controlled by the people.

January 20th 2017, will be remembered as the day the people became the rulers of this nation again.

The forgotten men and women of our country will be forgotten no longer.

Everyone is listening to you now.

You came by the tens of millions to become part of a historic movement the likes of which the world has never seen before.

At the center of this movement is a crucial conviction: that a nation exists to serve its citizens.

Americans want great schools for their children, safe neighborhoods for their families, and good jobs for themselves.

These are the just and reasonable demands of a righteous public.

But for too many of our citizens, a different reality exists: Mothers and children trapped in poverty in our inner cities; rusted-out factories scattered like tombstones across the landscape of our nation; an education system, flush with cash, but which leaves our young and beautiful students deprived of knowledge; and the crime and gangs and drugs that have stolen too many lives and robbed our country of so much unrealized potential.

This American carnage stops right here and stops right now.

We are one nation–and their pain is our pain. Their dreams are our dreams; and their success will be our success. We share one heart, one home, and one glorious destiny.

The oath of office I take today is an oath of allegiance to all Americans.

For many decades, we've enriched foreign industry at the expense of American industry;

Subsidized the armies of other countries while allowing for the very sad depletion of our military;

We've defended other nation's borders while refusing to defend our own;

And spent trillions of dollars overseas while America's infrastructure has fallen into disrepair and decay.

We've made other countries rich while the wealth, strength, and confidence of our country has disappeared over the horizon.

One by one, the factories shuttered and left our shores, with not even a thought about the millions upon millions of American workers left behind.

The wealth of our middle class has been ripped from their homes and then redistributed across the entire world.

But that is the past. And now we are looking only to the future.

We assembled here today are issuing a new decree to be heard in every city, in every foreign capital, and in every hall of power.

From this day forward, a new vision will govern our land.

From this moment on, it's going to be America First.

Every decision on trade, on taxes, on immigration, on foreign affairs, will be made to benefit American workers and American families.

We must protect our borders from the ravages of other countries making our products, stealing our companies, and destroying our jobs. Protection will lead to great prosperity and strength.

I will fight for you with every breath in my body–and I will never, ever let you down.

America will start winning again, winning like never before.

We will bring back our jobs. We will bring back our borders. We will bring back our wealth. And we will bring back our dreams.

We will build new roads, and highways, and bridges, and airports, and tunnels, and railways all across our wonderful nation.

We will get our people off of welfare and back to work–rebuilding our country with American hands and American labor.

We will follow two simple rules: Buy American and Hire American.

We will seek friendship and goodwill with the nations of the world–but we do so with the understanding that it is the right of all nations to put their own interests first.

We do not seek to impose our way of life on anyone, but rather to let it shine as an example for everyone to follow.

We will reinforce old alliances and form new ones–and unite the civilized world against Radical Islamic Terrorism, which we will eradicate completely from the face of the Earth.

At the bedrock of our politics will be a total allegiance to the United States of America, and through our loyalty to our country, we will rediscover our loyalty to each other.

When you open your heart to patriotism, there is no room for prejudice.

The Bible tells us, "how good and pleasant it is when God's people live together in unity."

We must speak our minds openly, debate our disagreements honestly, but always pursue solidarity.

When America is united, America is totally unstoppable.

There should be no fear–we are protected, and we will always be protected.

We will be protected by the great men and women of our military and law enforcement and, most importantly, we are protected by God.

Finally, we must think big and dream even bigger.

In America, we understand that a nation is only living as long as it is striving.

We will no longer accept politicians who are all talk and no action–constantly complaining but never doing anything about it.

The time for empty talk is over.

Now arrives the hour of action.

Do not let anyone tell you it cannot be done. No challenge can match the heart and fight and spirit of America.

We will not fail. Our country will thrive and prosper again.

We stand at the birth of a new millennium, ready to unlock the mysteries of space, to free the Earth from the miseries of disease, and to harness the energies, industries and technologies of tomorrow.

45

A new national pride will stir our souls, lift our sights, and heal our divisions.

It is time to remember that old wisdom our soldiers will never forget: that whether we are black or brown or white, we all bleed the same red blood of patriots, we all enjoy the same glorious freedoms, and we all salute the same great American Flag.

And whether a child is born in the urban sprawl of Detroit or the windswept plains of Nebraska, they look up at the same night sky, they fill their heart with the same dreams, and they are infused with the breath of life by the same almighty Creator.

So to all Americans, in every city near and far, small and large, from mountain to mountain, and from ocean to ocean, hear these words:

You will never be ignored again.

Your voice, your hopes, and your dreams, will define our American destiny. And your courage and goodness and love will forever guide us along the way.

Together, We Will Make America Strong Again.

We Will Make America Wealthy Again.

We Will Make America Proud Again.

We Will Make America Safe Again.

And, Yes, Together, We Will Make America Great Again. Thank you, God Bless You, And God Bless America.

Remarks in Joint Address to U.S. Congress
February 28, 2017
U.S. Capitol

Thank you very much. Mr. Speaker, Mr. Vice President, members of Congress, the First Lady of the United States (Applause) and citizens of America:

Tonight, as we mark the conclusion of our celebration of Black History Month, we are reminded of our nation's path towards civil rights and the work that still remains to be done. (Applause.) Recent threats targeting Jewish community centers and vandalism of Jewish cemeteries, as well as last week's shooting in Kansas City, remind us that while we may be a nation divided on policies, we are a country that stands united in condemning hate and evil in all of its very ugly forms. (Applause.)

Each American generation passes the torch of truth, liberty and justice in an unbroken chain all the way down to the present. That torch is now in our hands. And we will use it to light up the world. I am here tonight to deliver a message of unity and strength, and it is a message deeply delivered from my heart. A new chapter (Applause) of American Greatness is now beginning. A new national pride is sweeping across our nation. And a new surge of optimism is placing impossible dreams firmly within our grasp.

What we are witnessing today is the renewal of the American spirit. Our allies will find that America is once again ready to lead. (Applause.) All the nations of the world—friend or foe—will find that America is strong, America is proud, and America is free.

In nine years, the United States will celebrate the 250th anniversary of our founding—250 years since the day we declared our independence. It will be one of the great milestones in the history of the world. But what will America look like as we reach our 250th year? What kind of country will we leave for our children?

I will not allow the mistakes of recent decades past to define the course of our future. For too long, we've watched our middle class shrink as we've exported our jobs and wealth to foreign countries. We've financed and built one global project after another, but ignored the fates of our children in the inner cities of Chicago, Baltimore, Detroit, and so many other places throughout our land.

We've defended the borders of other nations while leaving our own borders wide open for anyone to cross and for drugs to pour in at a now unprecedented rate. And we've spent trillions and trillions of dollars overseas, while our infrastructure at home has so badly crumbled.

Then, in 2016, the Earth shifted beneath our feet. The rebellion started as a quiet protest, spoken by families of all colors and creeds—families who just wanted a fair shot for their children and a fair hearing for their concerns.

47

But then the quiet voices became a loud chorus as thousands of citizens now spoke out together, from cities small and large, all across our country. Finally, the chorus became an earthquake, and the people turned out by the tens of millions, and they were all united by one very simple, but crucial demand: that America must put its own citizens first. Because only then can we truly make America great again. (Applause.)

Dying industries will come roaring back to life. Heroic veterans will get the care they so desperately need. Our military will be given the resources its brave warriors so richly deserve. Crumbling infrastructure will be replaced with new roads, bridges, tunnels, airports and railways gleaming across our very, very beautiful land. Our terrible drug epidemic will slow down and, ultimately, stop. And our neglected inner cities will see a rebirth of hope, safety and opportunity. Above all else, we will keep our promises to the American people. (Applause.)

It's been a little over a month since my inauguration, and I want to take this moment to update the nation on the progress I've made in keeping those promises.

Since my election, Ford, Fiat-Chrysler, General Motors, Sprint, Softbank, Lockheed, Intel, Walmart and many others have announced that they will invest billions and billions of dollars in the United States, and will create tens of thousands of new American jobs. (Applause.)

The stock market has gained almost $3 trillion in value since the election on November 8th, a record. We've saved taxpayers hundreds of millions of dollars by bringing down the price of a fantastic—and it is a fantastic—new F-35 jet fighter, and we'll be saving billions more on contracts all across our government. We have placed a hiring freeze on non-military and non-essential federal workers.

We have begun to drain the swamp of government corruption by imposing a five-year ban on lobbying by executive branch officials and a lifetime ban (applause) thank you—and a lifetime ban on becoming lobbyists for a foreign government.

We have undertaken a historic effort to massively reduce job-crushing regulations, creating a deregulation task force inside of every government agency. (Applause.) And we're imposing a new rule which mandates that for every one new regulation, two old regulations must be eliminated. (Applause.) We're going to stop the regulations that threaten the future and livelihood of our great coal miners. (Applause.)

We have cleared the way for the construction of the Keystone and Dakota Access Pipelines (applause) thereby creating tens of thousands of jobs. And I've issued a new directive that new American pipelines be made with American steel. (Applause.)

We have withdrawn the United States from the job-killing Trans-Pacific Partnership. (Applause.) And with the help of Prime Minister Justin Trudeau, we have formed a council with our neighbors in Canada to help ensure that women entrepreneurs have access to the networks, markets and capital they need to start a business and live out their financial dreams. (Applause.)

To protect our citizens, I have directed the Department of Justice to form a Task Force on Reducing Violent Crime. I have further ordered the Departments of Homeland Security and Justice, along with the Department of State and the Director of National Intelligence, to coordinate an aggressive strategy to dismantle the criminal cartels that have spread all across our nation. (Applause.) We will stop the drugs from pouring into our country and poisoning our youth, and we will expand treatment for those who have become so badly addicted. (Applause.)

At the same time, my administration has answered the pleas of the American people for immigration enforcement and border security. (Applause.) By finally enforcing our immigration laws, we will raise wages, help the unemployed, save billions and billions of dollars, and make our communities safer for everyone. (Applause.) We want all Americans to succeed, but that can't happen in an environment of lawless chaos. We must restore integrity and the rule of law at our borders. (Applause.)

For that reason, we will soon begin the construction of a great, great wall along our southern border. (Applause.) As we speak tonight, we are removing gang members, drug dealers, and criminals that threaten our communities and prey on our very innocent citizens. Bad ones are going out as I speak, and as I promised throughout the campaign.

To any in Congress who do not believe we should enforce our laws, I would ask you this one question: What would you say to the American family that loses their jobs, their income, or their loved one because America refused to uphold its laws and defend its borders? (Applause.)

Our obligation is to serve, protect, and defend the citizens of the United States. We are also taking strong measures to protect our nation from radical Islamic terrorism. (Applause.) According to data provided by the Department of Justice, the vast majority of individuals convicted of terrorism and terrorism-related offenses since 9/11 came here from outside of our country. We have seen the attacks at home—from Boston to San Bernardino to the Pentagon, and, yes, even the World Trade Center.

We have seen the attacks in France, in Belgium, in Germany, and all over the world. It is not compassionate, but reckless to allow uncontrolled entry from places where proper vetting cannot occur. (Applause.) Those given the high honor of admission to the United States should support this country and love its people and its values. We cannot allow a beachhead of terrorism to form inside America. We cannot allow our nation to become a sanctuary for extremists. (Applause.)

That is why my administration has been working on improved vetting procedures, and we will shortly take new steps to keep our nation safe and to keep out those out who will do us harm. (Applause.)

As promised, I directed the Department of Defense to develop a plan to demolish and destroy ISIS—a network of lawless savages that have slaughtered Muslims and Christians, and men, and women, and children of all faiths and all beliefs. We will work with our allies, including our friends and allies in the Muslim world, to extinguish this vile enemy from our planet. (Applause.)

I have also imposed new sanctions on entities and individuals who support Iran's ballistic missile program, and reaffirmed our unbreakable alliance with the State of Israel. (Applause.)

Finally, I have kept my promise to appoint a justice to the United States Supreme Court, from my list of 20 judges, who will defend our Constitution. (Applause.)

I am greatly honored to have Maureen Scalia with us in the gallery tonight. (Applause.) Thank you, Maureen. Her late, great husband, Antonin Scalia, will forever be a symbol of American justice. To fill his seat, we have chosen Judge Neil Gorsuch, a man of incredible skill and deep devotion to the law. He was confirmed unanimously by the Court of Appeals, and I am asking the Senate to swiftly approve his nomination. (Applause.)

Tonight, as I outline the next steps we must take as a country, we must honestly acknowledge the circumstances we inherited. Ninety-four million Americans are out of the labor force. Over 43 million people are now living in poverty, and over 43 million Americans are on food stamps. More than one in five people in their prime working years are not working. We have the worst financial recovery in 65 years. In the last eight years, the past administration has put on more new debt than nearly all of the other Presidents combined.

We've lost more than one-fourth of our manufacturing jobs since NAFTA was approved, and we've lost 60,000 factories since China joined the World Trade Organization in 2001. Our trade deficit in goods with the world last year was nearly $800 billion dollars. And overseas we have inherited a series of tragic foreign policy disasters.

Solving these and so many other pressing problems will require us to work past the differences of party. It will require us to tap into the American spirit that has overcome every challenge throughout our long and storied history. But to accomplish our goals at home and abroad, we must restart the engine of the American economy—making it easier for companies to do business in the United States, and much, much harder for companies to leave our country. (Applause.)

Right now, American companies are taxed at one of the highest rates anywhere in the world. My economic team is developing historic tax reform that will reduce the tax rate on our companies so they can compete and thrive anywhere and with anyone. (Applause.) It will be a big, big cut.

At the same time, we will provide massive tax relief for the middle class. We must create a level playing field for American companies and our workers. We have to do it. (Applause.) Currently, when we ship products out of America, many other countries make us pay very high tariffs and taxes. But when foreign companies ship their products into America, we charge them nothing, or almost nothing.

I just met with officials and workers from a great American company, Harley-Davidson. In fact, they proudly displayed five of their magnificent motorcycles, made in the USA, on the front lawn of the White House. (Laughter and applause.) And they wanted me to ride one and I said, "No, thank you." (Laughter.)

At our meeting, I asked them, how are you doing, how is business? They said that it's good. I asked them further, how are you doing with other countries, mainly international sales? They told me—without even complaining, because they have been so mistreated for so long that they've become used to it—that it's very hard to do business with other countries because they tax our goods at such a high rate. They said that in the case of another country, they taxed their motorcycles at 100 percent. They weren't even asking for a change. But I am. (Applause.)

I believe strongly in free trade but it also has to be fair trade. It's been a long time since we had fair trade. The first Republican President, Abraham Lincoln, warned that the "abandonment of the protective policy by the American government ... will produce want and ruin among our people." Lincoln was right—and it's time we heeded his advice and his words. (Applause.) I am not going to let America and its great companies and workers be taken advantage of us any longer. They have taken advantage of our country. No longer. (Applause.)

I am going to bring back millions of jobs. Protecting our workers also means reforming our system of legal immigration. (Applause.) The current, outdated system depresses wages for our poorest workers, and puts great pressure on taxpayers. Nations around the world, like Canada, Australia and many others, have a merit-based immigration system. (Applause.) It's a basic principle that those seeking to enter a country ought to be able to support themselves financially. Yet, in America, we do not enforce this rule, straining the very public resources that our poorest citizens rely upon. According to the National Academy of Sciences, our current immigration system costs American taxpayers many billions of dollars a year.

Switching away from this current system of lower-skilled immigration, and instead adopting a merit-based system, we will have so many more benefits. It will save countless dollars, raise workers' wages, and help struggling families—including immigrant families—enter the middle class.

And they will do it quickly, and they will be very, very happy, indeed. (Applause.)

I believe that real and positive immigration reform is possible, as long as we focus on the following goals: To improve jobs and wages for Americans; to strengthen our nation's security; and to restore respect for our laws. If we are guided by the well-being of American citizens, then I believe Republicans and Democrats can work together to achieve an outcome that has eluded our country for decades. (Applause.)

Another Republican President, Dwight D. Eisenhower, initiated the last truly great national infrastructure program—the building of the Interstate Highway System. The time has come for a new program of national rebuilding. (Applause.) America has spent approximately $6 trillion in the Middle East—all the while our infrastructure at home is crumbling. With this $6 trillion, we could have rebuilt our country twice, and maybe even three times if we had people who had the ability to negotiate. (Applause.)

To launch our national rebuilding, I will be asking Congress to approve legislation that produces a $1 trillion investment in infrastructure of the United States—financed through both public and private capital—creating millions of new jobs. (Applause.) This effort will be guided by two core principles: buy American and hire American. (Applause.)

Tonight, I am also calling on this Congress to repeal and replace Obamacare—(applause)—with reforms that expand choice, increase access, lower costs, and, at the same time, provide better healthcare. (Applause.)

Mandating every American to buy government-approved health insurance was never the right solution for our country. (Applause.) The way to make health insurance available to everyone is to lower the cost of health insurance, and that is what we are going do. (Applause.)

Obamacare premiums nationwide have increased by double and triple digits. As an example, Arizona went up 116 percent last year alone. Governor Matt Bevin of Kentucky just said Obamacare is failing in his state—the state of Kentucky—and it's unsustainable and collapsing.

One-third of counties have only one insurer, and they are losing them fast. They are losing them so fast. They are leaving, and many Americans have no choice at all. There's no choice left. Remember when you were told that you could keep your doctor and keep your plan? We now know that all of those promises have been totally broken. Obamacare is collapsing, and we must act decisively to protect all Americans. (Applause.)

Action is not a choice, it is a necessity. So I am calling on all Democrats and Republicans in Congress to work with us to save Americans from this imploding Obamacare disaster. (Applause.)

Here are the principles that should guide the Congress as we move to create a better healthcare system for all Americans:

First, we should ensure that Americans with preexisting conditions have access to coverage, and that we have a stable transition for Americans currently enrolled in the healthcare exchanges. (Applause.)

Secondly, we should help Americans purchase their own coverage through the use of tax credits and expanded Health Savings Accounts—but it must be the plan they want, not the plan forced on them by our government. (Applause.)

Thirdly, we should give our great state governors the resources and flexibility they need with Medicaid to make sure no one is left out. (Applause.)

Fourth, we should implement legal reforms that protect patients and doctors from unnecessary costs that drive up the price of insurance, and work to bring down the artificially high price of drugs, and bring them down immediately. (Applause.)

And finally, the time has come to give Americans the freedom to purchase health insurance across state lines—(applause)—which will create a truly competitive national marketplace that will bring costs way down and provide far better care. So important.

Everything that is broken in our country can be fixed. Every problem can be solved. And every hurting family can find healing and hope.

Our citizens deserve this, and so much more—so why not join forces and finally get the job done, and get it done right? (Applause.) On this and so many other things, Democrats and Republicans should get together and unite for the good of our country and for the good of the American people. (Applause.)

My administration wants to work with members of both parties to make childcare accessible and affordable, to help ensure new parents that they have paid family leave—(applause)—to invest in women's health, and to promote clean air and clean water, and to rebuild our military and our infrastructure. (Applause.)

True love for our people requires us to find common ground, to advance the common good, and to cooperate on behalf of every American child who deserves a much brighter future.

An incredible young woman is with us this evening, who should serve as an inspiration to us all. Today is Rare Disease Day, and joining us in the gallery is a rare disease survivor, Megan Crowley. (Applause.)

Megan was diagnosed with Pompe disease, a rare and serious illness, when she was 15 months old. She was not expected to live past five. On receiving this news, Megan's dad, John, fought with everything he had to save the life of his precious child. He founded a company to look for a cure, and helped develop the drug that saved Megan's life. Today she is 20 years old and a sophomore at Notre Dame. (Applause.)

Megan's story is about the unbounded power of a father's love for a daughter. But our slow and burdensome approval process at the Food and Drug Administration keeps too many advances, like the one that saved Megan's life, from reaching those in need. If we slash the restraints, not just at the FDA but across our government, then we will be blessed with far more miracles just like Megan. (Applause.) In fact, our children will grow up in a nation of miracles.

But to achieve this future, we must enrich the minds and the souls of every American child. Education is the civil rights issue of our time. (Applause.) I am calling upon members of both parties to pass an education bill that funds school choice for disadvantaged youth, including millions of African American and Latino children. (Applause.) These families should be free to choose the public, private, charter, magnet, religious, or home school that is right for them. (Applause.)

Joining us tonight in the gallery is a remarkable woman, Denisha Merriweather. As a young girl, Denisha struggled in school and failed third grade twice. But then she was able to enroll in a private center for learning— a great learning center—with the help of a tax credit and a scholarship program.

Today, she is the first in her family to graduate, not just from high school, but from college. Later this year she will get her master's degree in social work. We want all children to be able to break the cycle of poverty just like Denisha. (Applause.)

But to break the cycle of poverty, we must also break the cycle of violence. The murder rate in 2015 experienced its largest single-year increase in nearly half a century. In Chicago, more than 4,000 people were shot last year alone, and the murder rate so far this year has been even higher. This is not acceptable in our society. (Applause.)

Every American child should be able to grow up in a safe community, to attend a great school, and to have access to a high-paying job. (Applause.) But to create this future, we must work with, not against—not against—the men and women of law enforcement. (Applause.) We must build bridges of cooperation and trust—not drive the wedge of disunity and, really, it's what it is, division. It's pure, unadulterated division. We have to unify.

Police and sheriffs are members of our community. They're friends and neighbors, they're mothers and fathers, sons and daughters—and they leave behind loved ones every day who worry about whether or not they'll come home safe and sound. We must support the incredible men and women of law enforcement. (Applause.)

And we must support the victims of crime. I have ordered the Department of Homeland Security to create an office to serve American victims. The office is called VOICE—Victims of Immigration Crime Engagement. We are providing a voice to those who have been ignored by our media and silenced by special interests. (Applause.) Joining us in the audience tonight are four very brave Americans whose government failed them. Their names are Jamiel Shaw, Susan Oliver, Jenna Oliver, and Jessica Davis.

Jamiel's 17-year-old son was viciously murdered by an illegal immigrant gang member who had just been released from prison. Jamiel Shaw, Jr. was an incredible young man, with unlimited potential who was getting ready to go to college where he would have excelled as a great college quarterback. But he never got the chance. His father, who is in the audience tonight, has become a very good friend of mine. Jamiel, thank you. Thank you. (Applause.)

Also with us are Susan Oliver and Jessica Davis. Their husbands, Deputy Sheriff Danny Oliver and Detective Michael Davis, were slain in the line of duty in California. They were pillars of their community. These brave men were viciously gunned down by an illegal immigrant with a criminal record and two prior deportations. Should have never been in our country.

Sitting with Susan is her daughter, Jenna. Jenna, I want you to know that your father was a hero, and that tonight you have the love of an entire country supporting you and praying for you. (Applause.)

To Jamiel, Jenna, Susan and Jessica, I want you to know that we will never stop fighting for justice. Your loved ones will never, ever be forgotten. We will always honor their memory. (Applause.)

Finally, to keep America safe, we must provide the men and women of the United States military with the tools they need to prevent war—if they must—they have to fight and they only have to win. (Applause.)

I am sending Congress a budget that rebuilds the military, eliminates the defense sequester—(applause)—and calls for one of the largest increases in national defense spending in American history. My budget will also increase funding for our veterans. Our veterans have delivered for this nation, and now we must deliver for them. (Applause.)

The challenges we face as a nation are great, but our people are even greater. And none are greater or braver than those who fight for America in uniform. (Applause.)

We are blessed to be joined tonight by Carryn Owens, the widow of a U.S. Navy Special Operator, Senior Chief William "Ryan" Owens. Ryan died as he lived: a warrior and a hero, battling against terrorism and securing our nation. (Applause.) I just spoke to our great General Mattis, just now, who reconfirmed that—and I quote—"Ryan was a part of a highly successful raid that generated large amounts of vital intelligence that will lead to many more victories in the future against our enemies." Ryan's legacy is etched into eternity. Thank you. (Applause.) And Ryan is looking down, right now—you know that—and he is very happy because I think he just broke a record. (Laughter and applause.)

For as the Bible teaches us, "There is no greater act of love than to lay down one's life for one's friends." Ryan laid down his life for his friends, for his country, and for our freedom. And we will never forget Ryan. (Applause.)

To those allies who wonder what kind of a friend America will be, look no further than the heroes who wear our uniform. Our foreign policy calls for a direct, robust and meaningful engagement with the world. It is American leadership based on vital security interests that we share with our allies all across the globe.

We strongly support NATO, an alliance forged through the bonds of two world wars that dethroned fascism, and a Cold War, and defeated communism. (Applause.)

But our partners must meet their financial obligations. And now, based on our very strong and frank discussions, they are beginning to do just that. In fact, I can tell you, the money is pouring in. Very nice. (Applause.) We expect our partners—whether in NATO, the Middle East, or in the Pacific—to take a direct and meaningful role in both strategic and military operations, and pay their fair share of the cost. Have to do that.

We will respect historic institutions, but we will respect the foreign rights of all nations, and they have to respect our rights as a nation also. (Applause.) Free nations are the best vehicle for expressing the will of the people, and America respects the right of all nations to chart their own path. My job is not to represent the world. My job is to represent the United States of America. (Applause.)

But we know that America is better off when there is less conflict, not more. We must learn from the mistakes of the past. We have seen the war and the destruction that have ravaged and raged throughout the world—all across the world. The only long-term solution for these humanitarian disasters, in many cases, is to create the conditions where displaced persons can safely return home and begin the long, long process of rebuilding. (Applause.)

America is willing to find new friends, and to forge new partnerships, where shared interests align. We want harmony and stability, not war and conflict. We want peace, wherever peace can be found.

America is friends today with former enemies. Some of our closest allies, decades ago, fought on the opposite side of these terrible, terrible wars. This history should give us all faith in the possibilities for a better world. Hopefully, the 250th year for America will see a world that is more peaceful, more just, and more free.

On our 100th anniversary, in 1876, citizens from across our nation came to Philadelphia to celebrate America's centennial. At that celebration, the country's builders and artists and inventors showed off their wonderful creations. Alexander Graham Bell displayed his telephone for the first time.

Remington unveiled the first typewriter. An early attempt was made at electric light. Thomas Edison showed an automatic telegraph and an electric pen. Imagine the wonders our country could know in America's 250th year. (Applause.)

Think of the marvels we can achieve if we simply set free the dreams of our people. Cures to the illnesses that have always plagued us are not too much to hope. American footprints on distant worlds are not too big a dream. Millions lifted from welfare to work is not too much to expect. And streets where mothers are safe from fear, schools where children learn in peace, and jobs where Americans prosper and grow are not too much to ask. (Applause.)

When we have all of this, we will have made America greater than ever before—for all Americans. This is our vision. This is our mission. But we can only get there together. We are one people, with one destiny. We all bleed the same blood. We all salute the same great American flag. And we all are made by the same God. (Applause.)

When we fulfill this vision, when we celebrate our 250 years of glorious freedom, we will look back on tonight as when this new chapter of American Greatness began. The time for small thinking is over. The time for trivial fights is behind us. We just need the courage to share the dreams that fill our hearts, the bravery to express the hopes that stir our souls, and the confidence to turn those hopes and those dreams into action.

From now on, America will be empowered by our aspirations, not burdened by our fears; inspired by the future, not bound by the failures of the past; and guided by our vision, not blinded by our doubts.

I am asking all citizens to embrace this renewal of the American spirit. I am asking all members of Congress to join me in dreaming big, and bold, and daring things for our country. I am asking everyone watching tonight to seize this moment. Believe in yourselves, believe in your future, and believe, once more, in America.

Thank you, God bless you, and God bless the United States. (Applause.)

Remarks by President Trump to the People of Poland
July 6, 2017
Krasiński Square, Warsaw, Poland

Hello, Poland! Thank you very much. My husband and I have enjoyed visiting your beautiful country. I want to thank President and Mrs. Duda for the warm welcome and their generous hospitality. I had the opportunity to visit the Copernicus Science Centre today, and found it not only informative but thoughtful, its mission, which is to inspire people to observe, experiment, ask questions, and seek answers.

I can think of no better purpose for such a wonderful science center. Thank you to all who were involved in giving us the tour, especially the children who made it such a wonderful experience.

As many of you know, a main focus of my husband's presidency is safety and security of the American people. I think all of us can agree people should be able to live their lives without fear, no matter what country they live in. That is my wish for all of us around the world. (Applause.)

Thank you again for this wonderful welcome to your very special country. Your kindness and gracious hospitality will not be forgotten. (Applause.)

And now it is my honor to introduce to you my husband, the President of the United States, Donald J. Trump. (Applause.)

PRESIDENT TRUMP: Thank you very much. That's so nice. The United States has many great diplomats, but there is truly no better ambassador for our country than our beautiful First Lady, Melania. Thank you, Melania. That was very nice. (Applause.)

We've come to your nation to deliver a very important message: America loves Poland, and America loves the Polish people. (Applause.) Thank you.

The Poles have not only greatly enriched this region, but Polish-Americans have also greatly enriched the United States, and I was truly proud to have their support in the 2016 election. (Applause.)

It is a profound honor to stand in this city, by this monument to the Warsaw Uprising, and to address the Polish nation that so many generations have dreamed of: a Poland that is safe, strong, and free. (Applause.)

President Duda and your wonderful First Lady, Agata, have welcomed us with the tremendous warmth and kindness for which Poland is known around the world. Thank you. (Applause.) My sincere—and I mean sincerely thank both of them. And to Prime Minister Syzdlo, a very special thanks also. (Applause.)

We are also pleased that former President Lech Walesa, so famous for leading the Solidarity Movement, has joined us today, also. (Applause.) Thank you. Thank you. Thank you.

On behalf of all Americans, let me also thank the entire Polish people for the generosity you have shown in welcoming our soldiers to your country. These soldiers are not only brave defenders of freedom, but also symbols of America's commitment to your security and your place in a strong and democratic Europe.

We are proudly joined on stage by American, Polish, British, and Romanian soldiers. Thank you. (Applause.) Thank you. Great job.

President Duda and I have just come from an incredibly successful meeting with the leaders participating in the Three Seas Initiative. To the citizens of this great region, America is eager to expand our partnership with you. We welcome stronger ties of trade and commerce as you grow your economies. And we are committed to securing your access to alternate sources of energy, so Poland and its neighbors are never again held hostage to a single supplier of energy. (Applause.)

Mr. President, I congratulate you, along with the President of Croatia, on your leadership of this historic Three Seas Initiative. Thank you. (Applause.)

This is my first visit to Central Europe as President, and I am thrilled that it could be right here at this magnificent, beautiful piece of land. It is beautiful. (Applause.) Poland is the geographic heart of Europe, but more importantly, in the Polish people, we see the soul of Europe. Your nation is great because your spirit is great and your spirit is strong. (Applause.)

For two centuries, Poland suffered constant and brutal attacks. But while Poland could be invaded and occupied, and its borders even erased from the map, it could never be erased from history or from your hearts. In those dark days, you have lost your land but you never lost your pride. (Applause.)

So it is with true admiration that I can say today, that from the farms and villages of your countryside to the cathedrals and squares of your great cities, Poland lives, Poland prospers, and Poland prevails. (Applause.)

Despite every effort to transform you, oppress you, or destroy you, you endured and overcame. You are the proud nation of Copernicus—think of that—(applause)—Chopin, Saint John Paul II. Poland is a land of great heroes. (Applause.) And you are a people who know the true value of what you defend.

The triumph of the Polish spirit over centuries of hardship gives us all hope for a future in which good conquers evil, and peace achieves victory over war.

For Americans, Poland has been a symbol of hope since the beginning of our nation. Polish heroes and American patriots fought side by side in our War of Independence and in many wars that followed. Our soldiers still serve together today in Afghanistan and Iraq, combating the enemies of all civilization.

For America's part, we have never given up on freedom and independence as the right and destiny of the Polish people, and we never, ever will. (Applause.)

Our two countries share a special bond forged by unique histories and national characters. It's a fellowship that exists only among people who have fought and bled and died for freedom. (Applause.)

The signs of this friendship stand in our nation's capital. Just steps from the White House, we've raised statues of men with names like Pułaski and Kościuszko. (Applause.) The same is true in Warsaw, where street signs carry the name of George Washington, and a monument stands to one of the world's greatest heroes, Ronald Reagan. (Applause.)

And so I am here today not just to visit an old ally, but to hold it up as an example for others who seek freedom and who wish to summon the courage and the will to defend our civilization. (Applause.) The story of Poland is the story of a people who have never lost hope, who have never been broken, and who have never, ever forgotten who they are. (Applause)

AUDIENCE: Donald Trump! Donald Trump! Donald Trump!

PRESIDENT TRUMP: Thank you. Thank you so much. Thank you. Thank you so much. Such a great honor. This is a nation more than one thousand years old. Your borders were erased for more than a century and only restored just one century ago.

In 1920, in the Miracle of Vistula, Poland stopped the Soviet army bent on European conquest. (Applause.) Then, 19 years later in 1939, you were invaded yet again, this time by Nazi Germany from the west and the Soviet Union from the east. That's trouble. That's tough.

Under a double occupation the Polish people endured evils beyond description: the Katyn forest massacre, the occupations, the Holocaust, the Warsaw Ghetto and the Warsaw Ghetto Uprising, the destruction of this beautiful capital city, and the deaths of nearly one in five Polish people. A vibrant Jewish population—the largest in Europe—was reduced to almost nothing after the Nazis systematically murdered millions of Poland's Jewish citizens, along with countless others, during that brutal occupation.

In the summer of 1944, the Nazi and Soviet armies were preparing for a terrible and bloody battle right here in Warsaw. Amid that hell on earth, the citizens of Poland rose up to defend their homeland. I am deeply honored to be joined on stage today by veterans and heroes of the Warsaw Uprising. (Applause.)

AUDIENCE: (Chanting.)

PRESIDENT TRUMP: What great spirit. We salute your noble sacrifice and we pledge to always remember your fight for Poland and for freedom. Thank you. Thank you. (Applause.)

This monument reminds us that more than 150,000 Poles died during that desperate struggle to overthrow oppression.

From the other side of the river, the Soviet armed forces stopped and waited. They watched as the Nazis ruthlessly destroyed the city, viciously murdering men, women, and children. They tried to destroy this nation forever by shattering its will to survive.

But there is a courage and a strength deep in the Polish character that no one could destroy. The Polish martyr, Bishop Michael Kozal, said it well: "More horrifying than a defeat of arms is a collapse of the human spirit."

Through four decades of communist rule, Poland and the other captive nations of Europe endured a brutal campaign to demolish freedom, your faith, your laws, your history, your identity—indeed the very essence of your culture and your humanity. Yet, through it all, you never lost that spirit. (Applause.) Your oppressors tried to break you, but Poland could not be broken. (Applause.)

And when the day came on June 2nd, 1979, and one million Poles gathered around Victory Square for their very first mass with their Polish Pope, that day, every communist in Warsaw must have known that their oppressive system would soon come crashing down. (Applause.) They must have known it at the exact moment during Pope John Paul II's sermon when a million Polish men, women, and children suddenly raised their voices in a single prayer. A million Polish people did not ask for wealth. They did not ask for privilege. Instead, one million Poles sang three simple words: "We Want God." (Applause.)

In those words, the Polish people recalled the promise of a better future. They found new courage to face down their oppressors, and they found the words to declare that Poland would be Poland once again.

As I stand here today before this incredible crowd, this faithful nation, we can still hear those voices that echo through history. Their message is as true today as ever. The people of Poland, the people of America, and the people of Europe still cry out "We want God." (Applause.)

Together, with Pope John Paul II, the Poles reasserted their identity as a nation devoted to God. And with that powerful declaration of who you are, you came to understand what to do and how to live. You stood in solidarity against oppression, against a lawless secret police, against a cruel and wicked system that impoverished your cities and your souls. And you won. Poland prevailed. Poland will always prevail. (Applause.)

AUDIENCE: Donald Trump! Donald Trump! Donald Trump!

PRESIDENT TRUMP: Thank you. You were supported in that victory over communism by a strong alliance of free nations in the West that defied tyranny. Now, among the most committed members of the NATO Alliance, Poland has resumed its place as a leading nation of a Europe that is strong, whole, and free.

A strong Poland is a blessing to the nations of Europe, and they know that. A strong Europe is a blessing to the West and to the world. (Applause.)

One hundred years after the entry of American forces into World War I, the transatlantic bond between the United States and Europe is as strong as ever and maybe, in many ways, even stronger.

This continent no longer confronts the specter of communism. But today we're in the West, and we have to say there are dire threats to our security and to our way of life. You see what's happening out there. They are threats. We will confront them. We will win. But they are threats. (Applause.)

AUDIENCE: Donald Trump! Donald Trump! Donald Trump!

PRESIDENT TRUMP: We are confronted by another oppressive ideology—one that seeks to export terrorism and extremism all around the globe. America and Europe have suffered one terror attack after another. We're going to get it to stop. (Applause.)

During a historic gathering in Saudi Arabia, I called on the leaders of more than 50 Muslim nations to join together to drive out this menace which threatens all of humanity. We must stand united against these shared enemies to strip them of their territory and their funding, and their networks, and any form of ideological support that they may have. While we will always welcome new citizens who share our values and love our people, our borders will always be closed to terrorism and extremism of any kind. (Applause.)

AUDIENCE: Donald Trump! Donald Trump! Donald Trump!

PRESIDENT TRUMP: We are fighting hard against radical Islamic terrorism, and we will prevail. We cannot accept those who reject our values and who use hatred to justify violence against the innocent.

Today, the West is also confronted by the powers that seek to test our will, undermine our confidence, and challenge our interests. To meet new forms of aggression, including propaganda, financial crimes, and cyberwarfare, we must adapt our alliance to compete effectively in new ways and on all new battlefields.

We urge Russia to cease its destabilizing activities in Ukraine and elsewhere, and its support for hostile regimes—including Syria and Iran—and to instead join the community of responsible nations in our fight against common enemies and in defense of civilization itself. (Applause.)

Finally, on both sides of the Atlantic, our citizens are confronted by yet another danger—one firmly within our control. This danger is invisible to some but familiar to the Poles: the steady creep of government bureaucracy that drains the vitality and wealth of the people. The West became great not because of paperwork and regulations but because people were allowed to chase their dreams and pursue their destinies.

Americans, Poles, and the nations of Europe value individual freedom and sovereignty. We must work together to confront forces, whether they come from inside or out, from the South or the East, that threaten over time to undermine these values and to erase the bonds of culture, faith and tradition that make us who we are. (Applause.) If left unchecked, these forces will undermine our courage, sap our spirit, and weaken our will to defend ourselves and our societies.

But just as our adversaries and enemies of the past learned here in Poland, we know that these forces, too, are doomed to fail if we want them to fail. And we do, indeed, want them to fail. (Applause.) They are doomed not only because our alliance is strong, our countries are resilient, and our power is unmatched. Through all of that, you have to say everything is true. Our adversaries, however, are doomed because we will never forget who we are. And if we don't forget who are, we just can't be beaten. Americans will never forget. The nations of Europe will never forget. We are the fastest and the greatest community. There is nothing like our community of nations. The world has never known anything like our community of nations.

We write symphonies. We pursue innovation. We celebrate our ancient heroes, embrace our timeless traditions and customs, and always seek to explore and discover brand-new frontiers.

We reward brilliance. We strive for excellence, and cherish inspiring works of art that honor God. We treasure the rule of law and protect the right to free speech and free expression. (Applause.)

We empower women as pillars of our society and of our success. We put faith and family, not government and bureaucracy, at the center of our lives. And we debate everything. We challenge everything. We seek to know everything so that we can better know ourselves. (Applause.)

And above all, we value the dignity of every human life, protect the rights of every person, and share the hope of every soul to live in freedom. That is who we are. Those are the priceless ties that bind us together as nations, as allies, and as a civilization.

What we have, what we inherited from our—and you know this better than anybody, and you see it today with this incredible group of people— what we've inherited from our ancestors has never existed to this extent before. And if we fail to preserve it, it will never, ever exist again. So we cannot fail.

This great community of nations has something else in common: In every one of them, it is the people, not the powerful, who have always formed the foundation of freedom and the cornerstone of our defense. The people have been that foundation here in Poland—as they were right here in Warsaw—and they were the foundation from the very, very beginning in America.

Our citizens did not win freedom together, did not survive horrors together, did not face down evil together, only to lose our freedom to a lack of pride and confidence in our values. We did not and we will not. We will never back down. (Applause.)

AUDIENCE: Donald Trump! Donald Trump! Donald Trump!

PRESIDENT TRUMP: As long as we know our history, we will know how to build our future. Americans know that a strong alliance of free, sovereign and independent nations is the best defense for our freedoms and for our interests. That is why my administration has demanded that all members of NATO finally meet their full and fair financial obligation.

As a result of this insistence, billions of dollars more have begun to pour into NATO. In fact, people are shocked. But billions and billions of dollars more are coming in from countries that, in my opinion, would not have been paying so quickly.

To those who would criticize our tough stance, I would point out that the United States has demonstrated not merely with words but with its actions that we stand firmly behind Article 5, the mutual defense commitment. (Applause.)

Words are easy, but actions are what matters. And for its own protection—and you know this, everybody knows this, everybody has to know this—Europe must do more. Europe must demonstrate that it believes in its future by investing its money to secure that future.

That is why we applaud Poland for its decision to move forward this week on acquiring from the United States the battle-tested Patriot air and missile defense system—the best anywhere in the world. (Applause.) That is also why we salute the Polish people for being one of the NATO countries that has actually achieved the benchmark for investment in our common defense. Thank you. Thank you, Poland. I must tell you, the example you set is truly magnificent, and we applaud Poland. Thank you. (Applause.)

We have to remember that our defense is not just a commitment of money, it is a commitment of will. Because as the Polish experience reminds us, the defense of the West ultimately rests not only on means but also on the will of its people to prevail and be successful and get what you have to have. The fundamental question of our time is whether the West has the will to survive. Do we have the confidence in our values to defend them at any cost? Do we have enough respect for our citizens to protect our borders? Do we have the desire and the courage to preserve our civilization in the face of those who would subvert and destroy it? (Applause.)

We can have the largest economies and the most lethal weapons anywhere on Earth, but if we do not have strong families and strong values, then we will be weak and we will not survive. (Applause.) If anyone forgets the critical importance of these things, let them come to one country that never has. Let them come to Poland. (Applause.) And let them come here, to Warsaw, and learn the story of the Warsaw Uprising.

When they do, they should learn about Jerusalem Avenue. In August of 1944, Jerusalem Avenue was one of the main roads running east and west through this city, just as it is today.

Control of that road was crucially important to both sides in the battle for Warsaw. The German military wanted it as their most direct route to move troops and to form a very strong front. And for the Polish Home Army, the ability to pass north and south across that street was critical to keep the center of the city, and the Uprising itself, from being split apart and destroyed.

Every night, the Poles put up sandbags amid machine gun fire—and it was horrendous fire—to protect a narrow passage across Jerusalem Avenue. Every day, the enemy forces knocked them down again and again and again. Then the Poles dug a trench. Finally, they built a barricade. And the brave Polish fighters began to flow across Jerusalem Avenue. That narrow passageway, just a few feet wide, was the fragile link that kept the Uprising alive.

Between its walls, a constant stream of citizens and freedom fighters made their perilous, just perilous, sprints. They ran across that street, they ran through that street, they ran under that street—all to defend this city. "The far side was several yards away," recalled one young Polish woman named Greta. That mortality and that life was so important to her. In fact, she said, "The mortally dangerous sector of the street was soaked in the blood. It was the blood of messengers, liaison girls, and couriers."

Nazi snipers shot at anybody who crossed. Anybody who crossed, they were being shot at. Their soldiers burned every building on the street, and they used the Poles as human shields for their tanks in their effort to capture Jerusalem Avenue. The enemy never ceased its relentless assault on that small outpost of civilization. And the Poles never ceased its defense.

The Jerusalem Avenue passage required constant protection, repair, and reinforcement, but the will of its defenders did not waver, even in the face of death. And to the last days of the Uprising, the fragile crossing never, ever failed. It was never, ever forgotten. It was kept open by the Polish people.

The memories of those who perished in the Warsaw Uprising cry out across the decades, and few are clearer than the memories of those who died to build and defend the Jerusalem Avenue crossing. Those heroes remind us that the West was saved with the blood of patriots; that each generation must rise up and play their part in its defense—(applause)—and that every foot of ground, and every last inch of civilization, is worth defending with your life.

Our own fight for the West does not begin on the battlefield—it begins with our minds, our wills, and our souls. Today, the ties that unite our civilization are no less vital, and demand no less defense, than that bare shred of land on which the hope of Poland once totally rested. Our freedom, our civilization, and our survival depend on these bonds of history, culture, and memory.

And today as ever, Poland is in our heart, and its people are in that fight. (Applause.) Just as Poland could not be broken, I declare today for the world

65

to hear that the West will never, ever be broken. Our values will prevail. Our people will thrive. And our civilization will triumph. (Applause.)

AUDIENCE: Donald Trump! Donald Trump! Donald Trump!

PRESIDENT TRUMP: Thank you. So, together, let us all fight like the Poles—for family, for freedom, for country, and for God.

Thank you. God Bless You. God bless the Polish people. God bless our allies. And God bless the United States of America.

Thank you. God bless you. Thank you very much. (Applause.)

Remarks at 72nd Session of the United Nations General Assembly
September 19, 2017
New York City

Mr. Secretary General, Mr. President, world leaders, and distinguished delegates: Welcome to New York. It is a profound honor to stand here in my home city, as a representative of the American people, to address the people of the world.

As millions of our citizens continue to suffer the effects of the devastating hurricanes that have struck our country, I want to begin by expressing my appreciation to every leader in this room who has offered assistance and aid. The American people are strong and resilient, and they will emerge from these hardships more determined than ever before.

Fortunately, the United States has done very well since Election Day last November 8th. The stock market is at an all-time high—a record. Unemployment is at its lowest level in 16 years, and because of our regulatory and other reforms, we have more people working in the United States today than ever before. Companies are moving back, creating job growth the likes of which our country has not seen in a very long time. And it has just been announced that we will be spending almost $700 billion on our military and defense.

Our military will soon be the strongest it has ever been. For more than 70 years, in times of war and peace, the leaders of nations, movements, and religions have stood before this assembly. Like them, I intend to address some of the very serious threats before us today but also the enormous potential waiting to be unleashed.

We live in a time of extraordinary opportunity. Breakthroughs in science, technology, and medicine are curing illnesses and solving problems that prior generations thought impossible to solve.

But each day also brings news of growing dangers that threaten everything we cherish and value. Terrorists and extremists have gathered strength and spread to every region of the planet. Rogue regimes represented in this body not only support terrorists but threaten other nations and their own people with the most destructive weapons known to humanity.

Authority and authoritarian powers seek to collapse the values, the systems, and alliances that prevented conflict and tilted the world toward freedom since World War II.

International criminal networks traffic drugs, weapons, people; force dislocation and mass migration; threaten our borders; and new forms of aggression exploit technology to menace our citizens.

To put it simply, we meet at a time of both of immense promise and great peril. It is entirely up to us whether we lift the world to new heights, or let it fall into a valley of disrepair.

We have it in our power, should we so choose, to lift millions from poverty, to help our citizens realize their dreams, and to ensure that new generations of children are raised free from violence, hatred, and fear.

This institution was founded in the aftermath of two world wars to help shape this better future. It was based on the vision that diverse nations could cooperate to protect their sovereignty, preserve their security, and promote their prosperity.

It was in the same period, exactly 70 years ago, that the United States developed the Marshall Plan to help restore Europe. Those three beautiful pillars—they're pillars of peace, sovereignty, security, and prosperity.

The Marshall Plan was built on the noble idea that the whole world is safer when nations are strong, independent, and free. As President Truman said in his message to Congress at that time, "Our support of European recovery is in full accord with our support of the United Nations. The success of the United Nations depends upon the independent strength of its members."

To overcome the perils of the present and to achieve the promise of the future, we must begin with the wisdom of the past. Our success depends on a coalition of strong and independent nations that embrace their sovereignty to promote security, prosperity, and peace for themselves and for the world.

We do not expect diverse countries to share the same cultures, traditions, or even systems of government. But we do expect all nations to uphold these two core sovereign duties: to respect the interests of their own people and the rights of every other sovereign nation. This is the beautiful vision of this institution, and this is foundation for cooperation and success.

Strong, sovereign nations let diverse countries with different values, different cultures, and different dreams not just coexist, but work side by side on the basis of mutual respect.

Strong, sovereign nations let their people take ownership of the future and control their own destiny. And strong, sovereign nations allow individuals to flourish in the fullness of the life intended by God.

In America, we do not seek to impose our way of life on anyone, but rather to let it shine as an example for everyone to watch. This week gives our country a special reason to take pride in that example. We are celebrating the 230th anniversary of our beloved Constitution—the oldest constitution still in use in the world today.

This timeless document has been the foundation of peace, prosperity, and freedom for the Americans and for countless millions around the globe whose own countries have found inspiration in its respect for human nature, human dignity, and the rule of law.

The greatest in the United States Constitution is its first three beautiful words. They are: "We the people."

Generations of Americans have sacrificed to maintain the promise of those words, the promise of our country, and of our great history. In America, the people govern, the people rule, and the people are sovereign. I was elected not to take power, but to give power to the American people, where it belongs.

In foreign affairs, we are renewing this founding principle of sovereignty. Our government's first duty is to its people, to our citizens—to serve their needs, to ensure their safety, to preserve their rights, and to defend their values.

As President of the United States, I will always put America first, just like you, as the leaders of your countries will always, and should always, put your countries first. (Applause.)

All responsible leaders have an obligation to serve their own citizens, and the nation-state remains the best vehicle for elevating the human condition.

But making a better life for our people also requires us to work together in close harmony and unity to create a more safe and peaceful future for all people.

The United States will forever be a great friend to the world, and especially to its allies. But we can no longer be taken advantage of, or enter into a one-sided deal where the United States gets nothing in return. As long as I hold this office, I will defend America's interests above all else.

But in fulfilling our obligations to our own nations, we also realize that it's in everyone's interest to seek a future where all nations can be sovereign, prosperous, and secure.

America does more than speak for the values expressed in the United Nations Charter. Our citizens have paid the ultimate price to defend our freedom and the freedom of many nations represented in this great hall. America's devotion is measured on the battlefields where our young men and women have fought and sacrificed alongside of our allies, from the beaches of Europe to the deserts of the Middle East to the jungles of Asia.

It is an eternal credit to the American character that even after we and our allies emerged victorious from the bloodiest war in history, we did not seek territorial expansion, or attempt to oppose and impose our way of life on others. Instead, we helped build institutions such as this one to defend the sovereignty, security, and prosperity for all.

For the diverse nations of the world, this is our hope. We want harmony and friendship, not conflict and strife. We are guided by outcomes, not ideology. We have a policy of principled realism, rooted in shared goals, interests, and values.

That realism forces us to confront a question facing every leader and nation in this room. It is a question we cannot escape or avoid. We will slide down the path of complacency, numb to the challenges, threats, and even wars that we face. Or do we have enough strength and pride to confront those dangers today, so that our citizens can enjoy peace and prosperity tomorrow?

If we desire to lift up our citizens, if we aspire to the approval of history, then we must fulfill our sovereign duties to the people we faithfully represent. We must protect our nations, their interests, and their futures. We must reject threats to sovereignty, from the Ukraine to the South China Sea. We must uphold respect for law, respect for borders, and respect for culture, and the peaceful engagement these allow. And just as the founders of this body intended, we must work together and confront together those who threaten us with chaos, turmoil, and terror.

The scourge of our planet today is a small group of rogue regimes that violate every principle on which the United Nations is based. They respect neither their own citizens nor the sovereign rights of their countries.

If the righteous many do not confront the wicked few, then evil will triumph. When decent people and nations become bystanders to history, the forces of destruction only gather power and strength.

No one has shown more contempt for other nations and for the wellbeing of their own people than the depraved regime in North Korea. It is responsible for the starvation deaths of millions of North Koreans, and for the imprisonment, torture, killing, and oppression of countless more.

We were all witness to the regime's deadly abuse when an innocent American college student, Otto Warmbier, was returned to America only to die a few days later. We saw it in the assassination of the dictator's brother using banned nerve agents in an international airport. We know it kidnapped a sweet 13-year-old Japanese girl from a beach in her own country to enslave her as a language tutor for North Korea's spies.

If this is not twisted enough, now North Korea's reckless pursuit of nuclear weapons and ballistic missiles threatens the entire world with unthinkable loss of human life.

It is an outrage that some nations would not only trade with such a regime, but would arm, supply, and financially support a country that imperils the world with nuclear conflict. No nation on earth has an interest in seeing this band of criminals arm itself with nuclear weapons and missiles.

The United States has great strength and patience, but if it is forced to defend itself or its allies, we will have no choice but to totally destroy North Korea. Rocket Man is on a suicide mission for himself and for his regime. The United States is ready, willing and able, but hopefully this will not be necessary. That's what the United Nations is all about; that's what the United Nations is for. Let's see how they do.

It is time for North Korea to realize that the denuclearization is its only acceptable future. The United Nations Security Council recently held two unanimous 15-0 votes adopting hard-hitting resolutions against North Korea, and I want to thank China and Russia for joining the vote to impose sanctions, along with all of the other members of the Security Council. Thank you to all involved.

But we must do much more. It is time for all nations to work together to isolate the Kim regime until it ceases its hostile behavior.

We face this decision not only in North Korea. It is far past time for the nations of the world to confront another reckless regime—one that speaks openly of mass murder, vowing death to America, destruction to Israel, and ruin for many leaders and nations in this room.

The Iranian government masks a corrupt dictatorship behind the false guise of a democracy. It has turned a wealthy country with a rich history and culture into an economically depleted rogue state whose chief exports are violence, bloodshed, and chaos. The longest-suffering victims of Iran's leaders are, in fact, its own people.

Rather than use its resources to improve Iranian lives, its oil profits go to fund Hezbollah and other terrorists that kill innocent Muslims and attack their peaceful Arab and Israeli neighbors. This wealth, which rightly belongs to Iran's people, also goes to shore up Bashar al-Assad's dictatorship, fuel Yemen's civil war, and undermine peace throughout the entire Middle East.

We cannot let a murderous regime continue these destabilizing activities while building dangerous missiles, and we cannot abide by an agreement if it provides cover for the eventual construction of a nuclear program. (Applause.) The Iran Deal was one of the worst and most one-sided transactions the United States has ever entered into. Frankly, that deal is an embarrassment to the United States, and I don't think you've heard the last of it—believe me.

It is time for the entire world to join us in demanding that Iran's government end its pursuit of death and destruction. It is time for the regime to free all Americans and citizens of other nations that they have unjustly detained. And above all, Iran's government must stop supporting terrorists, begin serving its own people, and respect the sovereign rights of its neighbors.

The entire world understands that the good people of Iran want change, and, other than the vast military power of the United States, that Iran's people are what their leaders fear the most. This is what causes the regime to restrict Internet access, tear down satellite dishes, shoot unarmed student protestors, and imprison political reformers.

Oppressive regimes cannot endure forever, and the day will come when the Iranian people will face a choice. Will they continue down the path of poverty, bloodshed, and terror? Or will the Iranian people return to the nation's proud roots as a center of civilization, culture, and wealth where their people can be happy and prosperous once again?

The Iranian regime's support for terror is in stark contrast to the recent commitments of many of its neighbors to fight terrorism and halt its financing.

In Saudi Arabia early last year, I was greatly honored to address the leaders of more than 50 Arab and Muslim nations. We agreed that all responsible nations must work together to confront terrorists and the Islamist extremism that inspires them.

We will stop radical Islamic terrorism because we cannot allow it to tear up our nation, and indeed to tear up the entire world.

We must deny the terrorists safe haven, transit, funding, and any form of support for their vile and sinister ideology. We must drive them out of our nations. It is time to expose and hold responsible those countries who support and finance terror groups like al Qaeda, Hezbollah, the Taliban and others that slaughter innocent people.

The United States and our allies are working together throughout the Middle East to crush the loser terrorists and stop the reemergence of safe havens they use to launch attacks on all of our people.

Last month, I announced a new strategy for victory in the fight against this evil in Afghanistan. From now on, our security interests will dictate the length and scope of military operations, not arbitrary benchmarks and timetables set up by politicians.

I have also totally changed the rules of engagement in our fight against the Taliban and other terrorist groups. In Syria and Iraq, we have made big gains toward lasting defeat of ISIS. In fact, our country has achieved more against ISIS in the last eight months than it has in many, many years combined.

We seek the de-escalation of the Syrian conflict, and a political solution that honors the will of the Syrian people. The actions of the criminal regime of Bashar al-Assad, including the use of chemical weapons against his own citizens—even innocent children—shock the conscience of every decent person. No society can be safe if banned chemical weapons are allowed to spread. That is why the United States carried out a missile strike on the airbase that launched the attack.

We appreciate the efforts of United Nations agencies that are providing vital humanitarian assistance in areas liberated from ISIS, and we especially thank Jordan, Turkey and Lebanon for their role in hosting refugees from the Syrian conflict.

The United States is a compassionate nation and has spent billions and billions of dollars in helping to support this effort. We seek an approach to refugee resettlement that is designed to help these horribly treated people, and which enables their eventual return to their home countries, to be part of the rebuilding process.

For the cost of resettling one refugee in the United States, we can assist more than 10 in their home region. Out of the goodness of our hearts, we offer financial assistance to hosting countries in the region, and we support recent agreements of the G20 nations that will seek to host refugees as close to their home countries as possible. This is the safe, responsible, and humanitarian approach.

For decades, the United States has dealt with migration challenges here in the Western Hemisphere. We have learned that, over the long term, uncontrolled migration is deeply unfair to both the sending and the receiving countries.

For the sending countries, it reduces domestic pressure to pursue needed political and economic reform, and drains them of the human capital necessary to motivate and implement those reforms.

For the receiving countries, the substantial costs of uncontrolled migration are borne overwhelmingly by low-income citizens whose concerns are often ignored by both media and government.

I want to salute the work of the United Nations in seeking to address the problems that cause people to flee from their homes. The United Nations and African Union led peacekeeping missions to have invaluable contributions in stabilizing conflicts in Africa. The United States continues to lead the world in humanitarian assistance, including famine prevention and relief in South Sudan, Somalia, and northern Nigeria and Yemen.

We have invested in better health and opportunity all over the world through programs like PEPFAR, which funds AIDS relief; the President's Malaria Initiative; the Global Health Security Agenda; the Global Fund to End Modern Slavery; and the Women Entrepreneurs Finance Initiative, part of our commitment to empowering women all across the globe.

We also thank—(applause)—we also thank the Secretary General for recognizing that the United Nations must reform if it is to be an effective partner in confronting threats to sovereignty, security, and prosperity. Too often the focus of this organization has not been on results, but on bureaucracy and process.

In some cases, states that seek to subvert this institution's noble aims have hijacked the very systems that are supposed to advance them. For example, it is a massive source of embarrassment to the United Nations that some governments with egregious human rights records sit on the U.N. Human Rights Council.

The United States is one out of 193 countries in the United Nations, and yet we pay 22 percent of the entire budget and more. In fact, we pay far more than anybody realizes. The United States bears an unfair cost burden, but, to be fair, if it could actually accomplish all of its stated goals, especially the goal of peace, this investment would easily be well worth it.

Major portions of the world are in conflict and some, in fact, are going to hell. But the powerful people in this room, under the guidance and auspices of the United Nations, can solve many of these vicious and complex problems.

The American people hope that one day soon the United Nations can be a much more accountable and effective advocate for human dignity and freedom around the world. In the meantime, we believe that no nation should have to bear a disproportionate share of the burden, militarily or financially. Nations of the world must take a greater role in promoting secure and prosperous societies in their own regions.

That is why in the Western Hemisphere, the United States has stood against the corrupt and destabilizing regime in Cuba and embraced the enduring dream of the Cuban people to live in freedom. My administration recently announced that we will not lift sanctions on the Cuban government until it makes fundamental reforms.

We have also imposed tough, calibrated sanctions on the socialist Maduro regime in Venezuela, which has brought a once thriving nation to the brink of total collapse.

The socialist dictatorship of Nicolas Maduro has inflicted terrible pain and suffering on the good people of that country. This corrupt regime destroyed a prosperous nation by imposing a failed ideology that has produced poverty and misery everywhere it has been tried. To make matters worse, Maduro has defied his own people, stealing power from their elected representatives to preserve his disastrous rule.

The Venezuelan people are starving and their country is collapsing. Their democratic institutions are being destroyed. This situation is completely unacceptable and we cannot stand by and watch.

As a responsible neighbor and friend, we and all others have a goal. That goal is to help them regain their freedom, recover their country, and restore their democracy. I would like to thank leaders in this room for condemning the regime and providing vital support to the Venezuelan people.

The United States has taken important steps to hold the regime accountable. We are prepared to take further action if the government of Venezuela persists on its path to impose authoritarian rule on the Venezuelan people.

We are fortunate to have incredibly strong and healthy trade relationships with many of the Latin American countries gathered here today. Our economic bond forms a critical foundation for advancing peace and prosperity for all of our people and all of our neighbors.

I ask every country represented here today to be prepared to do more to address this very real crisis. We call for the full restoration of democracy and political freedoms in Venezuela. (Applause.)

The problem in Venezuela is not that socialism has been poorly implemented, but that socialism has been faithfully implemented. (Applause.) From the Soviet Union to Cuba to Venezuela, wherever true socialism or communism has been adopted, it has delivered anguish and devastation and failure. Those who preach the tenets of these discredited ideologies only contribute to the continued suffering of the people who live under these cruel systems.

America stands with every person living under a brutal regime. Our respect for sovereignty is also a call for action. All people deserve a government that cares for their safety, their interests, and their wellbeing, including their prosperity.

In America, we seek stronger ties of business and trade with all nations of good will, but this trade must be fair and it must be reciprocal.

For too long, the American people were told that mammoth multinational trade deals, unaccountable international tribunals, and powerful global bureaucracies were the best way to promote their success. But as those promises flowed, millions of jobs vanished and thousands of factories disappeared. Others gamed the system and broke the rules. And our great middle class, once the bedrock of American prosperity, was forgotten and left behind, but they are forgotten no more and they will never be forgotten again.

While America will pursue cooperation and commerce with other nations, we are renewing our commitment to the first duty of every government: the duty of our citizens. This bond is the source of America's strength and that of every responsible nation represented here today.

If this organization is to have any hope of successfully confronting the challenges before us, it will depend, as President Truman said some 70 years ago, on the "independent strength of its members." If we are to embrace the opportunities of the future and overcome the present dangers together, there can be no substitute for strong, sovereign, and independent nations—nations that are rooted in their histories and invested in their destinies; nations that seek allies to befriend, not enemies to conquer; and most important of all, nations that are home to patriots, to men and women who are willing to sacrifice for their countries, their fellow citizens, and for all that is best in the human spirit.

In remembering the great victory that led to this body's founding, we must never forget that those heroes who fought against evil also fought for the nations that they loved.

Patriotism led the Poles to die to save Poland, the French to fight for a free France, and the Brits to stand strong for Britain.

Today, if we do not invest ourselves, our hearts, and our minds in our nations, if we will not build strong families, safe communities, and healthy societies for ourselves, no one can do it for us.

We cannot wait for someone else, for faraway countries or far-off bureaucrats—we can't do it. We must solve our problems, to build our prosperity, to secure our futures, or we will be vulnerable to decay, domination, and defeat.

The true question for the United Nations today, for people all over the world who hope for better lives for themselves and their children, is a basic one: Are we still patriots? Do we love our nations enough to protect their sovereignty and to take ownership of their futures? Do we revere them enough to defend their interests, preserve their cultures, and ensure a peaceful world for their citizens?

One of the greatest American patriots, John Adams, wrote that the American Revolution was "effected before the war commenced. The Revolution was in the minds and hearts of the people."

That was the moment when America awoke, when we looked around and understood that we were a nation. We realized who we were, what we valued, and what we would give our lives to defend. From its very first moments, the American story is the story of what is possible when people take ownership of their future.

The United States of America has been among the greatest forces for good in the history of the world, and the greatest defenders of sovereignty, security, and prosperity for all.

Now we are calling for a great reawakening of nations, for the revival of their spirits, their pride, their people, and their patriotism.

History is asking us whether we are up to the task. Our answer will be a renewal of will, a rediscovery of resolve, and a rebirth of devotion. We need to defeat the enemies of humanity and unlock the potential of life itself.

Our hope is a world and—world of proud, independent nations that embrace their duties, seek friendship, respect others, and make common cause in the greatest shared interest of all: a future of dignity and peace for the people of this wonderful Earth.

This is the true vision of the United Nations, the ancient wish of every people, and the deepest yearning that lives inside every sacred soul.

So let this be our mission, and let this be our message to the world: We will fight together, sacrifice together, and stand together for peace, for freedom, for justice, for family, for humanity, and for the almighty God who made us all.

Thank you. God bless you. God bless the nations of the world. And God bless the United States of America. Thank you very much. (Applause.)

Remarks at the 2017 Values Voter Summit
October 13, 2017
Omni Shoreham Hotel, Washington, D.C.

Thank you very much, Tony. (Applause.) Thank you. Thank you very much. (Applause.)

AUDIENCE: USA! USA! USA!

THE PRESIDENT: Thank you very much. You know, I've been here before. (Laughter.) You do know that. Before the big day on November 8th, I was here. I want to thank Mark Meadows and all of the folks that have really made this possible. And, Tony, tremendous guy.

We have some incredible people that we love and that we're involved with. So we all know that. And I'm being followed by Mr. Bennett—you know that, right? And I've been watching him say nice things about me before I knew him. Those are the ones I like—(laughter)—where they speak well of you before you know them. Right?

But I really want to thank everybody, and, Tony, for your extraordinary leadership of this organization. And I want to thank, also, Lawana, for your dedication to the faith community and to our nation. Work so hard.

It's great to be back here with so many friends at the 2017 Values Voter Summit, and we know what that means. (Applause.) We know what that means. America is a nation of believers, and together we are strengthened and sustained by the power of prayer. (Applause.)

As we gather for this tremendous event, our hearts remain sad and heavy for the victims of the horrific mass murder last week in Las Vegas. It was an act of pure evil.

But in the wake of such horror, we also witnessed the true character of our nation. A mother laid on top of her daughter to shield her from gunfire. A husband died to protect his beloved wife. Strangers rescued strangers, police officers—and you saw that, all of those incredible police officers, how brave they were, how great they were running into fire. (Applause.) And first responders, they rushed right into danger.

Americans defied evil and hatred with courage and love.

The men and women who risked their lives to save their fellow citizens gave proof to the words of this scripture: "The light shines in the darkness, and the darkness has not overcome it." (Applause)

All of America is praying for the wounded and the grieving, and we will be with them today and we will be with them forever. (Applause.) Just want to finish by saying that—really, and we understand it was so horrific to watch and so terrible—but to those who lost the ones they love: We know that we cannot erase your pain, but we promise to never, ever leave your side. We are one nation, and we all hurt together, we hope together, and we heal together. (Applause.)

We also stand with the millions of people who have suffered from the massive fires, which are right now raging in California, and the catastrophic hurricanes along the Gulf Coast, in Puerto Rico, the U.S. Virgin Islands. And I will tell you, I left Texas, and I left Florida, and I left Louisiana, and I went to Puerto Rico, and I met with the president [governor] of the Virgin Islands.

These are people that are incredible people. They've suffered gravely, and we'll be there. We're going to be there. We have, really—it's not even a question of a choice. We don't even want a choice. We're going to be there as Americans, and we love those people and what they've gone through. And they're all healing, and their states and territories are healing, and they're healing rapidly.

In the wake of the terrible tragedies of the past several weeks, the American people have responded with goodness and generosity, and bravery. You've seen it. The heroism of everyday citizens reminds us that the true strength of our nation is found in the hearts and souls of our people.

When America is unified, no force on Earth can break us apart. (Applause.) We love our families. We love our neighbors. We love our country. Everyone here today is brought together by the same shared and timeless values. We cherish the sacred dignity of every human life. (Applause.)

We believe in strong families and safe communities. We honor the dignity of work. (Applause.) We defend our Constitution. We protect religious liberty. (Applause.) We treasure our freedom. We are proud of our history. We support the rule of law and the incredible men and women of law enforcement. (Applause.) We celebrate our heroes, and we salute every American who wears the uniform. (Applause.)

We respect our great American flag. (Applause.) Thank you. Thank you. Thank you.

And we stand united behind the customs, beliefs and traditions that define who we are as a nation and as a people.

George Washington said that "religion and morality are indispensable" to America's happiness, really, prosperity and totally to its success. It is our faith and our values that inspires us to give with charity, to act with courage, and to sacrifice for what we know is right.

The American Founders invoked our Creator four times in the Declaration of Independence—four times. (Applause.) How times have changed. But you know what, now they're changing back again. Just remember that. (Applause.)

Benjamin Franklin reminded his colleagues at the Constitutional Convention to begin by bowing their heads in prayer.

Religious liberty is enshrined in the very first amendment of the Bill of Rights. And we all pledge allegiance to—very, very beautifully—"one nation under God." (Applause.)

78

This is America's heritage, a country that never forgets that we are all—all, every one of us—made by the same God in Heaven. (Applause.)

When I came to speak with you last year, I made you a promise. Well, one of the promises I made you was that I'd come back. See? (Applause.) And I don't even need your vote this year, right? That's even nicer. (Laughter.)

But I pledged that, in a Trump administration, our nation's religious heritage would be cherished, protected, and defended like you have never seen before. That's what's happening. That's what's happening. You see it every day. You're reading it.

So this morning I am honored and thrilled to return as the first sitting President to address this incredible gathering of friends—so many friends. (Applause.) So many friends. And I'll ask Tony and all our people that do such a great job in putting this event together—can I take next year off or not? (Laughter.) Or do I have to be back? I don't know.

AUDIENCE: No!

THE PRESIDENT: He's saying—they're saying no. Lawana is saying no. That means no. (Laughter.)

So I'm here to thank you for your support and to share with you how we are delivering on that promise, defending our shared values, and in so doing, how we are renewing the America we love.

In the last 10 months, we have followed through on one promise after another. (Applause.) I didn't have a schedule, but if I did have a schedule, I would say we are substantially ahead of schedule. (Applause.)

Some of those promises are to support and defend the Constitution. I appointed and confirmed a Supreme Court Justice in the mold of the late, great Justice Antonin Scalia, the newest member of the Supreme Court, Justice Neil Gorsuch. (Applause.)

To protect the unborn, I have reinstated a policy first put in place by President Ronald Reagan, the Mexico City Policy. (Applause.) To protect religious liberty, including protecting groups like this one, I signed a new executive action in a beautiful ceremony at the White House on our National Day of Prayer—(applause)—which day we made official. (Applause.)

Among many historic steps, the executive order followed through on one of my most important campaign promises to so many of you: to prevent the horrendous Johnson Amendment from interfering with your First Amendment rights. (Applause.) Thank you. We will not allow government workers to censor sermons or target our pastors or our ministers or rabbis. These are the people we want to hear from, and they're not going to be silenced any longer. (Applause.)

Just last week, based on this executive action, the Department of Justice issued a new guidance to all federal agencies to ensure that no religious group is ever targeted under my administration. It won't happen. (Applause.)

We have also taken action to protect the conscience rights of groups like the Little Sisters of the Poor. You know what they went through. (Applause.) What they went through—they were going through hell. And then all of the sudden they won. They said, how did that happen? (Laughter.)

We want to really point out that the Little Sisters of the Poor and other people of faith, they live by a beautiful calling, and we will not let bureaucrats take away that calling or take away their rights. (Applause.)

We are stopping cold the attacks on Judeo-Christian values. (Applause.) Thank you. Thank you very much. And something I've said so much during the last two years, but I'll say it again as we approach the end of the year. You know, we're getting near that beautiful Christmas season that people don't talk about anymore. (Laughter.) They don't use the word "Christmas" because it's not politically correct. You go to department stores, and they'll say, "Happy New Year" and they'll say other things. And it will be red, they'll have it painted, but they don't say it. Well, guess what? We're saying "Merry Christmas" again. (Applause.)

And as a Christmas gift to all of our hardworking families, we hope Congress will pass massive tax cuts for the American people. (Applause.) That includes increasing the child tax credit and expanding it to eliminate the marriage penalty. (Applause.) Because we know that the American family is the true bedrock of American life. So true. (Applause.) This is such an exciting event because we are really working very hard, and hopefully Congress will come through.

You saw what we did yesterday with respect to health care. It's step by step by step. (Applause.) And that was a very big step yesterday. Another big step was taken the day before yesterday. And one by one it's going to come down, and we're going to have great healthcare in our country. We're going to have great healthcare in our country. (Applause.) We're taking a little different route than we had hoped, because getting Congress—they forgot what their pledges were. (Laughter.) So we're going a little different route. But you know what? In the end, it's going to be just as effective, and maybe it will even be better. (Applause.)

For too long, politicians have tried to centralize the authority among the hands of a small few in our nation's capital. Bureaucrats think they can run your lives, overrule your values, meddle in your faith, and tell you how to live, what to say, and how to pray. But we know that parents, not bureaucrats, know best how to raise their children and create a thriving society. (Applause.)

We know that faith and prayer, not federal regulation—and, by the way, we are cutting regulations at a clip that nobody has ever seen before. Nobody. (Applause.) In nine months, we have cut more regulation than any President has cut during their term in office. So we are doing the job. (Applause.) And that is one of the major reasons, in addition to the enthusiasm for manufacturing and business and jobs—and the jobs are coming back.

That's one of the major reasons—regulation, what we've done—that the stock market has just hit an all-time historic high. (Applause.) That just on the public markets we've made, since Election Day, $5.2 trillion in value. Think of that: $5.2 trillion. (Applause.) And as you've seen, the level of enthusiasm is the highest it's ever been, and we have a 17-year low in unemployment. So we're doing, really, some work. (Applause.)

We know that it's the family and the church, not government officials, that know best how to create strong and loving communities. (Applause.) And above all else, we know this: In America, we don't worship government—we worship God. (Applause.) Inspired by that conviction, we are returning moral clarity to our view of the world and the many grave challenges we face.

This afternoon, in a little while, I'll be giving a speech on Iran, a terrorist nation like few others. And I think you're going to find it very interesting. (Applause.)

Yesterday, things happened with Pakistan, and I have openly said Pakistan took tremendous advantage of our country for many years, but we're starting to have a real relationship with Pakistan and they're starting to respect us as a nation again, and so are other nations. They're starting to respect the United States of America again, and I appreciate that. (Applause.) And I want to thank the leaders of Pakistan for what they've been doing.

In this administration, we will call evil by its name. (Applause.) We stand with our friends and allies, we forge new partnerships in pursuit of peace, and we take decisive action against those who would threaten our people with harm. (Applause.) And we will be decisive—because we know that the first duty of government is to serve its citizens. We are defending our borders, protecting our workers, and enforcing our laws. You see it every single day like you haven't seen it in many, many years—if you've seen it at all. (Applause.)

In protecting America's interests abroad, we will always support our cherished friend and partner, the State of Israel. (Applause.) We will confront the dangers that imperil our nation, our allies, and the world, including the threat of radical Islamic terrorism. (Applause.)

We have made great strides against ISIS—tremendous strides. I don't know if you've seen what's going on, but tremendous strides against ISIS. They never got hit like this before. (Laughter.)

AUDIENCE MEMBER: (Inaudible.)

THE PRESIDENT: Stand up. Stand up. Let me see—he's a rough guy. I can see it.

But they've been just ruthless and they've ruthlessly slaughtered innocent Christians, along with the vicious killing of innocent Muslims and other religious minorities. And we've made their lives very, very difficult—believe me. (Applause.)

We've done more against ISIS in nine months than the previous administration has done during its whole administration—by far, by far. (Applause.) And ISIS is now being dealt one defeat after another. We are confronting rogue regimes from Iran to North Korea, and we are challenging the communist dictatorship of Cuba and the socialist oppression of Venezuela. And we will not lift the sanctions on these repressive regimes until they restore political and religious freedom for their people. (Applause.)

All of these bad actors share a common enemy, the one force they cannot stop, the force deep within our souls, and that is the power of hope. That is why, in addition to our great military might, our enemies truly fear the United States. Because our people never lose faith, never give in, and always hope for a better tomorrow.

Last week, Melania and I were reminded of this in a powerful way when we traveled to Las Vegas. We visited a hospital where some of the survivors were recovering from absolutely horrific wounds. We met a young man named Brady Cook. He's 22 and a brand-new police officer. That night was Brady's second day in field training—his second day as a policeman, can you believe that? But when the shooting began, he did not hesitate. He acted with incredible courage, rushing into the hail of bullets, and he was badly shot in the shoulder.

This is what Brady said: "I didn't expect it, but it's what I signed up for. When stuff goes down, I want to be there to face evil and to protect the good, innocent people that need it." And here's a young guy, great guy—and second day. I said, Brady, don't worry about it, it's going to be easier from here. (Laughter and applause.) Brady is a hero, and he can't wait to get back on the job.

Several weeks before, when Hurricane Harvey hit Houston, a local furniture storeowner, who's known in Texas as "Mattress Mack," decided he had to help. When the rain began to flood the streets of the city, he sent out his furniture trucks to rescue the stranded. He brought them back to his stores, and gave them food and a clean, dry place to stay, even if it meant ruining countless dollars' worth of furniture.

As "Mattress Mack" put it, "My faith defines me, it's who I am." "We can afford [the cost] ... what we can't afford"—we can't—and he said this very strongly, "what we can't afford is to cause people to lose hope."

In Brady and Mack, we see the strength of the American spirit. This spirit of courage and compassion is all around us, every day. It is the heartbeat of our great nation. And despite certain coverage, that beat is stronger than it's ever been before. You see right through it. (Applause.) That beat is stronger than it's ever been.

We see this spirit in the men and women who selflessly enlist in our armed forces and, really, who go out and risk their lives for God and for country. And we see it in the mothers and the fathers who get up at the crack of dawn; they work two jobs and sometimes three jobs. They sacrifice every day for the future and—future of their children. They have to go out. They go out. They work. The future of their children is everything to them. They put it before everything. And they make sure that the future of their children has God involved in it. So important to them. (Applause.)

We see it in the church communities that come together to care for one another, to pray for each other, and to stand strong with each other in times of need.

The people who grace our lives, and fill our homes, and build our communities are the true strength of our nation, and the greatest hope for a better tomorrow.

As long as we have pride in our country, confidence in our future, and faith in our God, then America will prevail.

We will defeat every evil, overcome every threat, and meet every single challenge. We will defend our faith and protect our traditions. We will find the best in each other and in ourselves. We will pass on the blessings of liberty, and the glories of God, to our children. Our values will endure, our nation will thrive, our citizens will flourish, and our freedom will triumph.

Thank you to the Values Voter Summit. Such an incredible group of people you are. Thank you to all of the faithful here today. And thank you to the people of faith all across our nation and all over the world.

May God bless you. May God bless the United States of America. Thank you very much, everybody. (Applause.)

Ed Martin

Remarks before the National Assembly Building
November 7, 2017
Seoul, Republic of Korea

PRESIDENT TRUMP: Assembly Speaker Chung, distinguished members of this Assembly, ladies and gentlemen: Thank you for the extraordinary privilege to speak in this great chamber and to address your people on behalf of the people of the United States of America.

In our short time in your country, Melania and I have been awed by its ancient and modern wonders, and we are deeply moved by the warmth of your welcome.

Last night, President and Mrs. Moon showed us incredible hospitality in a beautiful reception at the Blue House. We had productive discussions on increasing military cooperation and improving the trade relationship between our nations on the principle of fairness and reciprocity.

Through this entire visit, it has been both our pleasure and our honor to create and celebrate a long friendship between the United States and the Republic of Korea.

This alliance between our nations was forged in the crucible of war, and strengthened by the trials of history. From the Inchon landings to Pork Chop Hill, American and South Korean soldiers have fought together, sacrificed together, and triumphed together.

Almost 67 years ago, in the spring of 1951, they recaptured what remained of this city where we are gathered so proudly today. It was the second time in a year that our combined forces took on steep casualties to retake this capital from the communists.

Over the next weeks and months, the men soldiered through steep mountains and bloody, bloody battles. Driven back at times, they willed their way north to form the line that today divides the oppressed and the free. And there, American and South Korean troops have remained together holding that line for nearly seven decades. (Applause.)

By the time the armistice was signed in 1953, more than 36,000 Americans had died in the Korean War, with more than 100,000 others very badly wounded. They are heroes, and we honor them. We also honor and remember the terrible price the people of your country paid for their freedom. You lost hundreds of thousands of brave soldiers and countless innocent civilians in that gruesome war.

Much of this great city of Seoul was reduced to rubble. Large portions of the country were scarred—severely, severely hurt—by this horrible war. The economy of this nation was demolished.

But as the entire world knows, over the next two generations something miraculous happened on the southern half of this peninsula. Family by family, city by city, the people of South Korea built this country into what is

84

today one of the great nations of the world. And I congratulate you. (Applause.) In less than one lifetime, South Korea climbed from total devastation to among the wealthiest nations on Earth.

Today, your economy is more than 350 times larger than what it was in 1960. Trade has increased 1,900 times. Life expectancy has risen from just 53 years to more than 82 years today.

Like Korea, and since my election exactly one year ago today, I celebrate with you. (Applause.) The United States is going through something of a miracle itself. Our stock market is at an all-time high. Unemployment is at a 17-year low. We are defeating ISIS. We are strengthening our judiciary, including a brilliant Supreme Court justice, and on, and on, and on.

Currently stationed in the vicinity of this peninsula are the three largest aircraft carriers in the world loaded to the maximum with magnificent F-35 and F-18 fighter jets. In addition, we have nuclear submarines appropriately positioned. The United States, under my administration, is completely rebuilding its military and is spending hundreds of billions of dollars to the newest and finest military equipment anywhere in the world being built, right now. I want peace through strength. (Applause.)

We are helping the Republic of Korea far beyond what any other country has ever done. And, in the end, we will work things out far better than anybody understands or can even appreciate. I know that the Republic of Korea, which has become a tremendously successful nation, will be a faithful ally of the United States very long into the future. (Applause.)

What you have built is truly an inspiration. Your economic transformation was linked to a political one. The proud, sovereign, and independent people of your nation demanded the right to govern themselves. You secured free parliamentary elections in 1988, the same year you hosted your first Olympics, after, you elected your first civilian president in more than three decades. And when the Republic you won faced financial crisis, you lined up by the millions to give your most prized possessions—your wedding rings, heirlooms, and gold "luck keys"—to restore the promise of a better future for your children. (Applause.)

Your wealth is measured in more than money—It is measured in achievements of the mind and achievements of spirit. Over the last several decades, your scientists and engineers—have engineered so many magnificent things. You've pushed the boundaries of technology, pioneered miraculous medical treatments, and emerged as leaders in unlocking the mysteries of our universe.

Korean authors penned roughly 40,000 books this year. Korean musicians fill concert halls all around the world. Young Korean students graduate from college at the highest rates of any country. And Korean golfers are some of the best on Earth. (Applause.)

Fact—and you know what I'm going to say—the Women's U.S. Open was held this year at Trump National Golf Club in Bedminster, New Jersey, and it just happened to be won by a great Korean golfer, Sung-hyun Park. An eighth of the top 10 players were from Korea. And the top four golfers—one, two, three, four—the top four were from Korea. Congratulations. (Applause.) Congratulations. And that's something. That is really something.

Here in Seoul, architectural wonders like the Sixty-Three Building and the Lotte World Tower—very beautiful—grace the sky and house the workers of many growing industries.

Citizens now help to feed the hungry, fight terrorism, and solve problems all over the world. And in a few months, you will host the world and you will do a magnificent job at the 23rd Olympic Winter Games. Good luck. (Applause.)

The Korean miracle extends exactly as far as the armies of free nations advanced in 1953—24 miles to the north. There, it stops; it all comes to an end. Dead stop. The flourishing ends, and the prison state of North Korea sadly begins.

Workers in North Korea labor grueling hours in unbearable conditions for almost no pay. Recently, the entire working population was ordered to work for 70 days straight, or else pay for a day of rest.

Families live in homes without plumbing, and fewer than half have electricity. Parents bribe teachers in hopes of saving their sons and daughters from forced labor. More than a million North Koreans died of famine in the 1990s, and more continue to die of hunger today.

Among children under the age of five, nearly 30 percent of afflicted—and are afflicted by stunted growth due to malnutrition. And yet, in 2012 and 2013, the regime spent an estimated $200 million—or almost half the money that it allocated to improve living standards for its people—to instead build even more monuments, towers, and statues to glorify its dictators.

What remains of the meager harvest of the North Korean economy is distributed according to perceived loyalty to a twisted regime. Far from valuing its people as equal citizens, this cruel dictatorship measures them, scores them, and ranks them based on the most arbitrary indications of their allegiance to the state. Those who score the highest in loyalty may live in the capital city. Those who score the lowest starve. A small infraction by one citizen, such as accidentally staining a picture of the tyrant printed in a discarded newspaper, can wreck the social credit rank of his entire family for many decades.

An estimated 100,000 North Koreans suffer in gulags, toiling in forced labor, and enduring torture, starvation, rape, and murder on a constant basis.

In one known instance, a 9-year-old boy was imprisoned for 10 years because his grandfather was accused of treason. In another, a student was beaten in school for forgetting a single detail about the life of Kim Jong-un.

Soldiers have kidnapped foreigners and forced them to work as language tutors for North Korean spies.

In the part of Korea that was a stronghold for Christianity before the war, Christians and other people of faith who are found praying or holding a religious book of any kind are now detained, tortured, and in many cases, even executed.

North Korean women are forced to abort babies that are considered ethnically inferior. And if these babies are born, the newborns are murdered.

One woman's baby born to a Chinese father was taken away in a bucket. The guards said it did not "deserve to live because it was impure."

So why would China feel an obligation to help North Korea?

The horror of life in North Korea is so complete that citizens pay bribes to government officials to have themselves exported abroad as slaves. They would rather be slaves than live in North Korea.

To attempt to flee is a crime punishable by death. One person who escaped remarked, "When I think about it now, I was not a human being. I was more like an animal. Only after leaving North Korea did I realize what life was supposed to be."

And so, on this peninsula, we have watched the results of a tragic experiment in a laboratory of history. It is a tale of one people, but two Koreas. One Korea in which the people took control of their lives and their country, and chose a future of freedom and justice, of civilization, and incredible achievement. And another Korea in which leaders imprison their people under the banner of tyranny, fascism, and oppression. The result of this experiment are in, and they are totally conclusive.

When the Korean War began in 1950, the two Koreas were approximately equal in GDP per capita. But by the 1990s, South Korea's wealth had surpassed North Korea's by more than 10 times. And today, the South's economy is over 40 times larger. You started the same a short while ago, and now you're 40 times larger. You're doing something right.

Considering the misery wrought by the North Korean dictatorship, it is no surprise that it has been forced to take increasingly desperate measures to prevent its people from understanding this brutal contrast.

Because the regime fears the truth above all else, it forbids virtually all contact with the outside world. Not just my speech today, but even the most commonplace facts of South Korean life are forbidden knowledge to the North Korean people. Western and South Korean music is banned. Possession of foreign media is a crime punishable by death. Citizens spy on fellow citizens, their homes are subject to search at any time, and their every action is subject to surveillance. In place of a vibrant society, the people of North Korea are bombarded by state propaganda practically every waking hour of the day.

North Korea is a country ruled as a cult. At the center of this military cult is a deranged belief in the leader's destiny to rule as parent protector over a conquered Korean Peninsula and an enslaved Korean people.

The more successful South Korea becomes, the more decisively you discredit the dark fantasy at the heart of the Kim regime.

In this way, the very existence of a thriving South Korean republic threatens the very survival of the North Korean dictatorship.

This city and this assembly are living proof that a free and independent Korea not only can, but does stand strong, sovereign, and proud among the nations of the world. (Applause.)

Here, the strength of the nation does not come from the false glory of a tyrant. It comes from the true and powerful glory of a strong and great people—the people of the Republic of Korea—a Korean people who are free to live, to flourish, to worship, to love, to build, and to grow their own destiny.

In this Republic, the people have done what no dictator ever could—you took, with the help of the United States, responsibility for yourselves and ownership of your future. You had a dream—a Korean dream—and you built that dream into a great reality.

In so doing, you performed the miracle on the Hahn that we see all around us, from the stunning skyline of Seoul to the plains and peaks of this beautiful landscape. You have done it freely, you have done it happily, and you have done it in your own very beautiful way.

This reality—this wonderful place—your success is the greatest cause of anxiety, alarm, and even panic to the North Korean regime. That is why the Kim regime seeks conflict abroad—to distract from total failure that they suffer at home.

Since the so-called armistice, there have been hundreds of North Korean attacks on Americans and South Koreans. These attacks have included the capture and torture of the brave American soldiers of the USS Pueblo, repeated assaults on American helicopters, and the 1969 drowning [downing] of a U.S. surveillance plane that killed 31 American servicemen. The regime has made numerous lethal incursions in South Korea, attempted to assassinate senior leaders, attacked South Korean ships, and tortured Otto Warmbier, ultimately leading to that fine young man's death.

All the while, the regime has pursued nuclear weapons with the deluded hope that it could blackmail its way to the ultimate objective. And that objective we are not going to let it have. We are not going to let it have. All of Korea is under that spell, divided in half. South Korea will never allow what's going on in North Korea to continue to happen.

The North Korean regime has pursued its nuclear and ballistic missile programs in defiance of every assurance, agreement, and commitment it has made to the United States and its allies. It's broken all of those commitments.

After promising to freeze its plutonium program in 1994, it repeated [reaped] the benefits of the deal and then—and then immediately continued its illicit nuclear activities.

In 2005, after years of diplomacy, the dictatorship agreed to ultimately abandon its nuclear programs and return to the Treaty on Non-Proliferation. But it never did. And worse, it tested the very weapons it said it was going to give up. In 2009, the United States gave negotiations yet another chance, and offered North Korea the open hand of engagement. The regime responded by sinking a South Korean Navy ship, killing 46 Korean sailors. To this day, it continues to launch missiles over the sovereign territory of Japan and all other neighbors, test nuclear devices, and develop ICBMs to threaten the United States itself. The regime has interpreted America's past restraint as weakness. This would be a fatal miscalculation. This is a very different administration than the United States has had in the past.

Today, I hope I speak not only for our countries, but for all civilized nations, when I say to the North: Do not underestimate us, and do not try us. We will defend our common security, our shared prosperity, and our sacred liberty.

We did not choose to draw here, on this peninsula—(applause)—this magnificent peninsula—the thin line of civilization that runs around the world and down through time. But here it was drawn, and here it remains to this day. It is the line between peace and war, between decency and depravity, between law and tyranny, between hope and total despair. It is a line that has been drawn many times, in many places, throughout history. To hold that line is a choice free nations have always had to make. We have learned together the high cost of weakness and the high stakes of its defense.

America's men and women in uniform have given their lives in the fight against Nazism, imperialism, Communism and terrorism.

America does not seek conflict or confrontation, but we will never run from it. History is filled with discarded regimes that have foolishly tested America's resolve.

Anyone who doubts the strength or determination of the United States should look to our past, and you will doubt it no longer. We will not permit America or our allies to be blackmailed or attacked. We will not allow American cities to be threatened with destruction. We will not be intimidated. And we will not let the worst atrocities in history be repeated here, on this ground, we fought and died so hard to secure. (Applause.)

That is why I have come here, to the heart of a free and flourishing Korea, with a message for the peace-loving nations of the world: The time for excuses is over. Now is the time for strength. If you want peace, you must stand strong at all times. (Applause.) The world cannot tolerate the menace of a rogue regime that threatens with nuclear devastation.

All responsible nations must join forces to isolate the brutal regime of North Korea—to deny it and any form—any form of it. You cannot support, you cannot supply, you cannot accept. We call on every nation, including China and Russia, to fully implement U.N. Security Council resolutions, downgrade diplomatic relations with the regime, and sever all ties of trade and technology.

It is our responsibility and our duty to confront this danger together— because the longer we wait, the greater the danger grows, and the fewer the options become. (Applause.) And to those nations that choose to ignore this threat, or, worse still, to enable it, the weight of this crisis is on your conscience.

I also have come here to this peninsula to deliver a message directly to the leader of the North Korean dictatorship: The weapons you are acquiring are not making you safer. They are putting your regime in grave danger. Every step you take down this dark path increases the peril you face.

North Korea is not the paradise your grandfather envisioned. It is a hell that no person deserves. Yet, despite every crime you have committed against God and man, we are ready to offer, and we will do that—we will offer a path to a much better future. It begins with an end to the aggression of your regime, a stop to your development of ballistic missiles, and complete, verifiable, and total denuclearization. (Applause.)

A sky-top view of this peninsula shows a nation of dazzling light in the South and a mass of impenetrable darkness in the North. We seek a future of light, prosperity, and peace. But we are only prepared to discuss this brighter path for North Korea if its leaders cease their threats and dismantle their nuclear program.

The sinister regime of North Korea is right about only one thing: The Korean people do have a glorious destiny, but they could not be more wrong about what that destiny looks like. The destiny of the Korean people is not to suffer in the bondage of oppression, but to thrive in the glory of freedom. (Applause.)

What South Koreans have achieved on this peninsula is more than a victory for your nation. It is a victory for every nation that believes in the human spirit. And it is our hope that, someday soon, all of your brothers and sisters of the North will be able to enjoy the fullest of life intended by God.

Your republic shows us all of what is possible. In just a few decades, with only the hard work, courage, and talents of your people, you turned this war-torn land into a nation blessed with wealth, rich in culture, and deep in spirit. You built a home where all families can flourish and where all children can shine and be happy.

This Korea stands strong and tall among the great community of independent, confident, and peace-loving nations. We are nations that respect our citizens, cherish our liberty, treasure our sovereignty, and control our own destiny. We affirm the dignity of every person and embrace the full potential of every soul. And we are always prepared to defend the vital interests of our people against the cruel ambition of tyrants.

Together, we dream of a Korea that is free, a peninsula that is safe, and families that are reunited once again. We dream of highways connecting North and South, of cousins embracing cousins, and this nuclear nightmare replaced with the beautiful promise of peace.

Until that day comes, we stand strong and alert. Our eyes are fixed to the North, and our hearts praying for the day when all Koreans can live in freedom. (Applause.)

Thank you. (Applause.) God Bless You. God Bless the Korean people. Thank you very much. Thank you. (Applause.)

Remarks on Tax Reform and the Economy
November 30, 2017
St. Charles, Missouri

THE PRESIDENT: I told you that we would be saying, merry Christmas again, right? And it's great to be back in Missouri—a sign of a lot of good things because you're doing really well.

And I want to thank Governor Greitens and Attorney General Hawley, who—by the way, Josh—where's Josh? Josh, our next senator. Where is he? He's going to be a great senator. And he wants to see a major tax cut. I think I can speak for him, right? And your current senator does not want to see a tax cut. That's not good. That's not good. She wants your taxes to go up.

Secretary Mnuchin, who's doing such a fantastic job—thank you—and Linda McMahon. Everybody knows Administrator—small business, became a big business under Linda. She's helping a lot of people. Thank you very much, Linda.

I especially want to thank Missouri's incredible congressional delegation: Sam Graves—where's Sam? You all here? Yeah. They all flew in with me. They wouldn't miss that flight. Vicky Hartzler. Vicky, thank you. Thank you, Vicky.

Billy Long, who I think was my first endorser in the entire country, practically, Billy, right? Thank you, Billy.

Blaine Luetkemeyer. Blaine, thank you, Blaine. And he was great on television today. I watched him—I got up early and I watched you on—that was a good interview. Thank you. He's very much in favor of tax cuts.

Jason Smith and Ann Wagner. Thank you, Jason. Thank you, Ann.

And, you know, I have two others. I have a lot of faith in Faith, Sally Faith. Where's Sally, your mayor? Hi, Sally. Thanks, Sally. And Eric Schmitt, Missouri state treasurer. Thank you. Thank you, Eric. You're doing a great job.

Just three months ago, we came to this state to launch our plan to bring back Main Street by cutting taxes for American families and small businesses. Today, I've come back to this incredible state to spend an afternoon with its amazing citizens—you are amazing—to help push our plan for historic tax cuts right across that finish line. We're going to do that.

With your help, we can usher in a thrilling new era of opportunity and growth for this nation that we love so much. Tax cuts have already passed the House of Representatives. Big ones. Big ones. The eyes of the world now turn to the United States Senate.

A successful vote in the Senate this week will bring us one giant step closer to delivering an incredible victory for the American people. Massive tax cuts and reform. I don't even mention the word reform because people don't know exactly what we're talking about.

You know, for years, they have not been able to get tax cuts—many, many years, since Reagan. And the problem was they talked about tax reform, not tax cuts. I said, don't call it "reform," call it "tax cuts and reform." So every once in awhile we'll add the name "reform." But it's tax cuts.

We cannot sit—Right? The Governor agrees.

We cannot sit idly by and watch ourselves losing in competition to other countries as they continue to take away our jobs because their tax codes are more competitive and less burdensome than ours. That's why we must cut our taxes, reduce economic burdens, and restore America's competitive edge. We're going to do that, too. And it's already happening. Look what's happening with our markets. People get it.

If we do this, then America will win again like never, ever before. A vote to cut taxes is a vote to put America first again. We want to do that. We want to put America first again. It's time to take care of our workers, to protect our communities, and to rebuild our great country.

You know, we've spent almost $7 trillion in the Middle East over the last 16 years—$7 trillion. Now, I'm taking care of it. We're doing numbers like ISIS has never seen before. We're wiping them out—terrorists, they're bad.

And all of that, but we've spent almost $7 trillion. We could have rebuilt our country four times over. And we're going to start spending here. We're going to start spending here.

And with that being said, we're going to protect our country, whether it's North Korea or any—but we're going to protect our country like never before. We're going to build up our military and make our product here and make our planes, and our boats, and our everything here. But we're going to build up our military.

But we've got to start focusing on our country. That's why I'm saying America first. Make America great again—you've never heard that expression. All those hats. All those—they've never heard that expression before.

Oh, that was a good expression and it's a true expression and it's already happening and long ahead of schedule. And in fact, today, some numbers came out that people haven't seen in many, many years.

This beautiful city of St. Charles is the perfect place to deliver the message that I want to deliver. It's the place where America's past and future come to life on its historic brick-lined Main Street. Nice street, do you agree?

It was along these very streets that, in 1804, the great American explorers, Lewis and Clark, gathered their final supplies before setting out on their very historic expedition of discovery. I have to say, I didn't really know that until two days ago.

See? See, now the world is watching. Look at all the fake news back there. They're all—

93

AUDIENCE: Booo—

THE PRESIDENT: They're all watching.

Today, more than two centuries later, a new generation of American pioneers begins its own adventure, gathering inside the startups and the storefronts of main streets across the country, blazing new trails into totally uncharted territory of business and technology, and once again leading our nation into a future of limitless potential.

That's what we have in this country. We have the greatest people. It's the greatest country. I love this country so much.

Our country was not treated properly for a long time. We're treating it properly. We're treating it with love and with this. You got to treat it with this.

And today, just as it's always been, Main Street is the heart of our economy, the soul of our community, and the birthplace of American dreams.

But over the years, crippling taxes, massive regulation, and totally disastrous trade deals—oh, the trade deals. Oh, I get a headache thinking about who made these deals. One after another. WTO, NAFTA, the wonderful deal with South Korea—remember, they said it's going to produce 200,000 jobs? And it did, for South Korea. Didn't produce—we lost 200,000 jobs. It turned some of our businesses' main streets into empty ghost towns. You see what's happened.

Now we have a once-in-a-lifetime opportunity to restore American prosperity and reclaim America's great destiny. We've already made tremendous progress—far greater than I would have thought. I will tell you this in a non-braggadocious way—there has never been a 10-month President that has accomplished what we have accomplished. That I can tell you. That I can tell you.

Today, again, the stock market has reached another record, all-time high. The unemployment rate nationwide is the lowest it's been in 17 years—and 13 states this year have seen unemployment drop to the lowest levels in the history of their state. And I hate to tell you, but Missouri happens to be one of them.

We've created nearly 2 million jobs—2 million jobs, think of that. We used to lose millions. Now we've created 2 million jobs since I won the election. And, I want to say, since you won the election. I didn't win the election; you won the election.

And we will create countless more if we can sustain the 3 percent growth rate we have achieved for the past two quarters. But we're going to do much better than that. Remember I used to say, we can hit 4 and we can hit 3? And they were all saying, forget it, forget it. It was 1.2. It was doing terribly. We were flat. We were even. In all fairness, the stock market was going this way.

And now, we're hitting numbers that nobody thought possible, certainly not in this time. And the numbers going up are going to be much better than anybody anticipates. In fact, they're going to say that Trump is the opposite of an exaggerator—the exact opposite. They're going to start saying, Governor, that he ought to be a little bit more optimistic because his predictions were low, can you believe it?

You know, a year and a half ago, they were saying, oh, he can't do that. Now they're saying, hm, that was quick.

But by the way, the Commerce Department announced this morning that our GDP—that's the big one—in the third quarter, grew even faster than they reported previously. They made a mistake, they were too low. They had it at 3 percent. By the way, 3 percent—did you ever think you'd hear that in less than a year?

AUDIENCE: No!

THE PRESIDENT: And now it comes in at 3.3 percent, which is the largest increase in many years.

And if we didn't have the hurricanes, we would have been at 4 percent. The hurricanes were devastating. And I said, they're worth a point. They said they were worth like .006, but I said they were worth a point. We would have been at 4 percent, maybe even over 4 percent, but we had hurricanes.

We took care of them. In Texas and Florida, they did a great, great job—amazing job, tremendous leadership. And we're very proud.

Puerto Rico has been a very tough situation because of the fact that it was in very, very bad shape before the storms ever hit. But they're doing well there and it's healing and it's getting better. And we're getting them power, and all of the things that they have to have.

But I want to tell you there are a lot of brave people in every state. We have great, great people, and it's our number one resource, believe me. Really great.

But in order to achieve this bright and glowing future, the Senate must pass those tax cuts. Bring Main Street roaring back—and that's what's going to happen. This was all done without the tax cuts, and I'm not sure that people even believe the tax cuts. I want to see what happens.

And the big day will be either tomorrow or the next day. I would say do it now. We're ready. I said to the Republicans—and I want to tell you, these are good people. They really want a—I know they get hit hard, the senators and the congressmen—but they're all working hard. It's not so easy. It's complicated stuff. It's not so easy.

But we had an incredible session yesterday. And I think we're there. That's why I said, let's do—can we do the vote today? What do I know? I'm a business guy. Can we do the vote now? Well, they said, how about Friday? I said, I don't want to wait until Friday. Right, Billy? I said, Billy, can we do the vote? Get me the vote.

Well, Billy has already passed it, so—and then what happens, if it passes it goes into this beautiful committee—this beautiful—I call it a pot. And we mix it up, and we stir it up, and we bring all the best things out, and you're going to have something, I predict, that will be really, really special.

So, right now—really is.

So right now, America's tax code is a total dysfunctional mess. The current system has cost our nation millions of American jobs, trillions and trillions of dollars, and billions of hours wasted on paperwork and compliance. It is riddled with loopholes that let some special interests— Including myself, in all fairness. This is going to cost me a fortune, this thing—believe me.

Believe me, this is not good for me. Me, it's not so—I have some very wealthy friends—not so happy with me, but that's okay. You know, I keep hearing Schumer, "This is for the wealthy." Well, if it is, my friends don't know about it. I have to explain why.

Now it is great for companies, because companies are going to bring back jobs. And we're lowering the rates vary substantially. But right now, we're bringing the rates down from 35 percent—which is totally non-competitive. The highest industrialized nation in the world, by far, and we're bringing it all the way down to 20 percent.

But that's good for everybody in the room, whether you have company or whether you want a job, because we're going to bring back jobs.

And what we've had is a massive giveaway to foreign countries, which encourage businesses to relocate offshore. And you've seen what's happened.

Before this—this is, really, I'm most proud, because, as bad as our tax code is, we have Toyota, we have big car companies coming back in, building plants in Michigan and other places. We have a lot of businesses coming back in, and they see what's happening. They see what's going on.

That's why they're doing—our current code is a giant—and really it is— it's a self-inflicted economic wound. It's been that way for so many years and nobody wanted to do anything about it.

But all that will change and it will change immediately if Congress sends a tax cut and reform bill. The biggest tax cut in the history of our country— bigger than Reagan. If they send it to my desk, I promise all of the people in this room—my friends, so many friends in this room. It's a great state. I promise you I will sign it. I promise. I will not veto that bill. There will be no veto.

Under the plan moving forward in the Senate, a typical family of four earning $75,000, as an example, will see their taxes go down by as much as $2,000. That's a lot.

Now, we're doing that not just to help people. We're doing that because it helps our country. You're going to take that $2,000 and maybe you'll save some, and you're going to spend some. And we're going to make product back in our country again. It's going to be made here—going to be made elsewhere. But it's going to be made here. We're opening up plants. We're opening up factories, and we're going to be great to small business. Wait until you see the final product. Wait until you see what finally comes out in what I call the mixer.

The beating heart of our plan is a tax cut for working families. That's what it is. We're going to make sure—that you keep more of your hard-earned money. We're going to make sure, also, that you have a job that you want. You're going to have choice. In education we now have choice. Good word. Here you're going to have a choice. You're not just going to have one—you're going to have a choice of many jobs. People are moving back into our country.

Under our plan, the first $12,000 of income earned by a single individual will be totally income-tax-free—zero. And a married couple won't pay one dime of income tax on their first $24,000 of income—zero.

Our plan will significantly increase the child tax credit and make it available to more middle-class families because the single most important investment our nation can make is in our children. Do we agree? You agree? You better agree.

Families will also benefit from a new credit for other dependents like a child in college, or an elderly loved one. We have our mothers, our fathers. You have your grandparents. You have people that are elderly that have done a fantastic job. They've grown old. You want to help them. Now we are going to help you help them.

We're also going to eliminate tax breaks and complex loopholes taken advantage of by the wealthy. Who are they? I don't know. I think my accountants are going crazy right now. It's all right. Hey, look, I'm President. I don't care. I don't care anymore. I don't care.

Some of my wealthy friends care. Me? I don't care. This is a higher calling. Do we agree? As Hillary said, what difference does it make? It made a difference. It made a big difference. It made a big, big difference.

We want a tax code that is simple and fair, and that's for all Americans. The plan that senators will be voting on this week—hopefully as soon as possible—closes the loopholes that corporations use to shift their profits to tax havens, and it eliminates deductions for CEO salaries over $1 million. You see what some of these people are making—a little ridiculous.

I'm driving up their stock. They're making a fortune. Then they go to their board, and they tell everybody what a great job they're doing. But what am I going to do? And many of them, honestly, I don't like. Oh, some of these bankers I don't like them, and they're making a fortune, and it's one of those things.

Steve knows a couple of them that I'm talking about, doesn't he? They say what a great job they do. Right now anybody could do their job because we're making it easy for them because we're giving them a great and strong economy. And because we've cut regulations more than any President in the history of this country by far, and that's for full terms. That's not for 10 months.

And it allows builders to build, and it allows farmers to farm. You know what I've done for farmers. Where if you had a little puddle in the middle of your field, you go to jail if you touch it, right? You know what I'm talking about. Not anymore. Not anymore. Not anymore.

And it allows bankers to lend. It allows bankers to lend again. So many people came up to me, and they said, we had a 20-year relationship with a bank. We never had a default. We never had a bad loan. Now we go back to the bank, and they say, we can't do business with you anymore.

Because they don't qualify, even though they're better than the people that do qualify. It's incredible. But we're back to the strong days of our banks. And not the days of trouble—pre-that—we're back to the—where bankers can make loans and community bankers can make great loans to good people.

You saw what happened recently where the certain agency or bureau that was causing so much trouble to lenders, where they could not lend. They just couldn't lend. It was devastating. They were going out of business. Well, we're taking care of that. We've already taken care of a big part of it, and yesterday you saw we won the lawsuit. So that's going to be taken care of automatically. Got to get back to business.

Our focus is on helping the folks who work in the mailrooms and machine shops of America—the plumbers, the carpenters, the cops, the teachers, the truck drivers, the pipefitters—the people that like me best. Actually, the rich people actually don't like me, which is sort of interesting.

And that's fine. You know what? I like that trade. But really, the people that like me best are those people—the workers. They're the people I understand the best. Those are the people I grew up with. Those are the people I worked on construction sites with.

All of the people who give their best each and every day to take care of their family and the country that they love—these are incredible people. They came out to vote for me. They came out to vote for us. People that worked hard, two jobs, three jobs, that hadn't voted in many years because they never had anybody they wanted to vote for.

And they came out—I'll never forget, in Tennessee, a great congressman told me—they had early voting—said, I'll tell you what, we just went through four days of early voting. At that time, it was Mr. Trump. Now they say, Mr. President. But it was Mr. Trump.

He said, and if the other parts of the country are like what's happening in Tennessee—people are coming from all over Tennessee. They haven't voted in years, and now they've got Trump shirts and they've got Trump hats, and they've got Trump-Pence, and they've got everything Trump and Trump-Pence.

And he said, I've never seen anything like it, and I've been a politician for a lot of years. And if it's anything like Tennessee, you're going to have one hell of a victory. It turned out to be a lot like Tennessee, so .... And it turned out to be a lot like Missouri. That I can tell you. Because we had a big one here.

And I promised Josh that, when he gets it going—and he's got it in very good shape, from what I hear, he's a popular—everybody said, Josh, got to be Josh. Everyone who saw me—I said, who's going to run against her? Josh, Josh. I said, Josh, when you're ready, you have my word, I'm going to come here and campaign with you. We got to get you in. Okay? Got to get you in.

It's not enough for the middle class to keep getting by; we want them to start getting way ahead. We're going to have them start getting way ahead.

Under our plan, middle-class families will not only see their tax bill go down, they will see their incomes go up by an average of around $4,000. And that's because we're going to cut taxes on American businesses so they will compete for workers, they'll raise salaries. The business is going to be happy and the workers are going to be happy and the country is going to be a happy place.

Although, we're going to have very strong borders. Please remember that, okay? Please remember.

AUDIENCE MEMBER: Build the wall.

THE PRESIDENT: We're going to have the wall. Don't worry about it, we're going to have the wall. We don't forget that wall. A lot of people say, now that he got elected, is he going to build the wall? The answer is, absolutely—more so, I think more so.

It's not easy dealing with the Democrats. They want to have people pour into our country—illegals. They don't care where the hell they come from. They want to have them pour into our country, they want to raise your taxes, they don't want to take care of your military, and all they're good at, frankly, is obstructing. They want to obstruct.

But you know what? They may obstruct, but we have gotten through all of the obstruction so far. We'll keep it going, believe me.

Today, America has one of the least competitive tax rates on planet Earth—60 percent. Think of that: 60 percent higher than the average in the developed world. So our taxes are 60 percent higher.

On my recent trip to Asia, every single one of the countries I visited, even those with communist governments, have slashed its corporate tax rates

99

and slashed them dramatically. And it's very tough competition anyway. But when their taxes are a lot lower, it really makes it very tough.

And that trip was a tremendous success. You know, we brought back $250 billion in contracts. That's going to be over a trillion dollars very soon. That's a good week and a half's work. Boeing came back with contracts. So many of our companies came back, and I'm very proud of them. And we're doing great.

But at the same time, we're going to fix trade because trade is unfair. We're getting killed on trade. So we're going to fix our trade. Unless anybody would like to continue with this horrible situation that we have.

AUDIENCE: Booo.

THE PRESIDENT: Our plan gets America from the back of the pack and it'll bring us right to number one, where we were for years but where we haven't been for decades. We're going to be right back at number one.

And we're going to work on trade, but we're also going to work on military. When we defend nations that are very wealthy, and we do it for almost nothing, I say, why are we defending them? We love them. I won't mention names, but there are a lot of them. We love them. They're wealthy.

One of them has a cash flow that they say is unsustainable, it's so large. Think of that. How would you like to have an unsustainable cash flow? They don't know what to do with their money. And we defend them. It's going to change, folks. We're going to defend them, but they're going to treat us fairly. And they're going to pay for their defense. Does that make sense?

And a lot of this is from many, many years ago, when we defended a defeated country and then they became strong and they became rich and we just kept the same defense. What happened? Why didn't anybody go in and negotiate?

And when I was in Asia, I spoke to a couple of the countries about it, and they looked like this. Do you know what this is? That means they know they're getting away with murder and they got to start helping us out, okay? So if you don't mind, I'll start bringing that up with some of our good friends.

We're going to lower our tax rate to the very competitive number of 20 percent, as I said. And we're going to create jobs and factories will be pouring into this country, and they already are starting. A lot of people think it's going to happen. I don't want to say anything. I'm not going to talk about it. I thought we had healthcare, and we will have healthcare. It's going to happen. As soon as we get the taxes, we work on the healthcare, we're going to happen. Because we thought we had the votes and something happened a little strange—that's okay.

When you lose by one vote, then it's called—you go back. You know, some people said, oh, you failed with healthcare. I said, what do you mean we failed? We didn't fail. And by the way, what happened—what happened

100

is Obama took a long time—years—to get Obamacare, right? Again, ten months? We've had two runs at it. We're coming closer, closer. I think now we have a plan that's going to be great. But we're not talking about it until after taxes. And then we take care of healthcare.

Then we will have done tax cuts, the biggest in history; healthcare, phenomenal healthcare. I know you don't want this—welfare reform. Does anybody want welfare reform? And infrastructure. But welfare reform—I see it and I've talked to people. I know people, they work three jobs and they live next to somebody who doesn't work at all. And the person who's not working at all and has no intention of working at all is making more money and doing better than the person that's working his and her ass off. And it's not going to happen. Not going to happen.

So we're going to go into welfare reform, unless Billy doesn't want it. Billy, am I okay in saying that I speak for you? He said, yes.

AUDIENCE MEMBER: We love you, Billy.

THE PRESIDENT: You got a lot of friends out there, Bill.

Well, we'll also cut taxes for the millions of small businesses that file as individuals, and that's going to come out of the hopper. It's getting there and it's going to be better and better. We're reducing the tax burden on businesses of all sizes and of every, single kind.

As a candidate, I pledged to fight for American jobs. I think it's possibly the number one reason I got elected. And I think we've done a lot better, at this point, than anybody ever even thought possible. Think of that, two million jobs since the election—two million more jobs in this country since the election. Nobody expected that. Nobody expected that. Excuse me, I didn't even expect that.

But you cut those regulations and you give people spirit and incentive. And when you have the highest ratings, in terms of confidence, that the country has had in many, many years—maybe ever—things happen.

The tax cut will mean more companies moving to America, staying in America, and hiring American workers right here. So that's so important, right?

Small business groups across our nation, retailers, restaurants, manufacturers, grocers, contractors support this plan. We have tremendous support for this plan. Tremendous. Because these massive tax cuts will be rocket fuel—Little Rocket Man—rocket fuel for the American economy. He is a sick puppy.

Cassandra Porlier—where is she? Where is Cassandra? She's around here. Hello, Cassandra. I met you back there.

She and her mother, Teri—hi, Teri—they own a jewelry store on Main Street right here in St. Charles. They make really beautiful handmade jewelry. I got to see some of it. I would have taken it in my previous life. But now if I do, they don't like that. We're not allowed to take jewelry, right?

But they make it right here in the heartland. It's beautiful. Our tax plan will ensure that Cassandra can keep growing her business, keep creating jobs, keep giving back to the community that she loves, and just make her more and more successful.

I assume you like that, right? Good.

Randy Schilling is also here. Where's Randy? Randy—hello, Randy. He's the founder of O.P.O.—that's an interesting name. It's called O.P.O. Startups and a member to dozens of small businesses in the St. Charles area. He's a mentor. He really mentors a lot of the businesses, and he's respected.

He also did a terrific job renovating the old post office on Main Street, something I know something about—old post offices. Did he do a good job, by the way? I hear.

They said yes, Randy. If he did a bad job, I'm going to stop right now and just say, good luck, Randy. They said you did a good job. I know you did.

Randy knows firsthand how the high tax burden is holding America's small businesses back, and our tax cut plan will unleash them to thrive like never before. He understands our plan, which will provide relief from the horrible, crushing, unfair estate tax, also known to many as the death tax.

We want to make it easier for loving families to pass on their life's work to their children. Be nice. Be very nice, right?

That's a tough one. The Democrats fight that one I think harder than any other thing that we're doing. They fight the death tax. They don't want it. They don't like it. They don't want it. It's one of those things. But that is one of the hardest things. I have to be—I see people right here. They're obviously very rich, and they love their children, right, in this group? They love their children. They're very rich. They want to pass on what they have without having to have the kids sell the property, mortgage up half of it. But the biggest problem we have on that one, these Democrats are being brutal. And I call them obstructionists, but they want to stop the estate tax. They want to stop the death tax from being rescinded. But we're going to try our best on that one.

Our economy will receive another enormous boost as trillions of dollars in wealth that's parked overseas will be able to come back to our country.

Now, this one that's interesting because for years Republicans and Democrats agreed. You have Apple, and you have these great companies having billions and billions of dollars overseas. Now who doesn't want the money to come back?

But to show you the lack of leadership that this country had in the past, the Republicans want it, and the Democrats want it. And nothing ever happened. You could have passed that one easy. In fact, we're just throwing it into this bill. I could have had a separate bill on that one—I think. Don't you agree, fellas? I could have had a separate bill on that one and gotten it passed in record time. But I figured I'd put it here because it is actually popular.

But it used to be $2.5 trillion. You know what that is? Trillion. Money you can't bring back in. It's prohibitive—both in complexity and in the amount of tax you have to pay. So nobody brings back in—$2.5 trillion. But $2.5 [trillion] I've been saying for six years. I think now it's $4 trillion to $5 trillion. All that money is coming back into the United States, and it's going to be invested in our country, instead of sitting and helping others. We want our own help.

That's sort of an easy one. Last year, American multinational companies left more than 70 percent of their foreign profits overseas because the current tax system penalizes them for bringing that money back home. They actually get penalized. Our plan switches to a territorial tax system that encourages companies to return their profits to America—right here to the United States—where that money belongs going back to work for you. Territorial.

If we want America to thrive in the 21st century, then we must stop running from the competition. And instead, we must start totally winning and winning and winning again. Remember when I used to say: We're going to win so much. We're going to win—that the people of Missouri are going to go to your governor, and they're going to say, Governor, please, go see the President. We can't stand winning so much. Remember I used to say that? Right? I used to say it, and that's what's happening. That's what's happening.

And then the governor is going to come to that beautiful historic Oval Office. He's going to say to me, Mr. President, the people of Missouri cannot stand all this winning. They don't want to win so much. They love the old way where they had lousy job numbers, lousy economic numbers, lousy—yeah, they loved it. Please, Mr. President, please, not—and I'll say, Governor, I don't care what they say in Missouri, we're going to keep winning and winning and winning. Remember? That's right.

I used to say that. I had fun with that. But we are winning. We're winning again. We're winning a lot bigger than anyone ever thought possible for such a short period of time.

For too long, our tax code has incentivized companies to leave our country in search of lower tax rates. It happens. Many, many companies—they're going to Ireland. They're going all over. They're going all over Asia. But they're stopping because they now want to take advantage of what's happening and what we're about to pass, hopefully.

My administration rejects the offshoring model. In other words, let's build a factory in another country. Isn't that wonderful? That really helps us a lot. Fire everybody, and let's build a product, and let's send it in, without tax, back into the United States.

That model doesn't work for me. It never worked, and it shouldn't have worked for any of our other past Presidents, believe me.

Our new model is the American model. Call it the Trump model, where we build it here. As much as possible, we build it here. Simply put, our tax plan is anti-offshoring and 100 percent worker, 100 percent worker, 100 percent pro-America.

Under the American model, we're reducing burdens on our businesses as long as they do business in our country. Okay? They do business here.

Now, we love Mexico. It's a wonderful place. But I don't like when our car companies move to Mexico, fire everybody, build the same car in Mexico, send it through our borders with no taxes, no nothing, and we buy the car. Same price. We buy the car.

In the meantime, what do we get out of it? We get no tax and we get unemployment all over. That's stopping. So now the plants are starting to move back. And now there's a price to pay when they do that little number on us. That's how we will all succeed and we grow together as one team, one people, as one American family.

This week's vote can be the beginning of the next great chapter for the American worker.

To summarize: Our plan cuts taxes for the working and middle-income families; it nearly doubles the amount of income taxed at the rate of zero; it lowers tax rate; it expands the child tax credit; it provides relief from the estate tax, also known as the death tax; it cuts small business taxes; it reduces the corporate rate from 35 percent all the way down to 20 percent; and it provides a one-time low tax rate to return corporate money parked overseas—trillions and trillions of dollars.

This is the right plan. This is the right time. We have a moment in time. The Republicans have the Senate. The Republicans have the House. The Republicans have the White House. It's very unusual. It's very unusual.

This is our chance to free our economy from our workers—from the terrible tax burdens. We have workers that are so burdened with taxes. We're freeing our workers from those terrible burdens.

Republicans in Congress campaigned on cutting taxes. We also campaigned on repeal and replace. It's going to happen. It's going to happen. Take your time, it's going to happen—going to happen.

Many Democrats have promised tax cuts that don't mean anything because they really want major tax increases. Senator Claire McCaskill—have you ever heard of her?

AUDIENCE: Booo.

THE PRESIDENT: She is doing you a tremendous disservice. She wants your taxes to go up. She's weak on crime, she's weak on borders, she's weak on illegal immigration, and she's weak on the military. Other than that, I think she's doing a fantastic job.

104

But now comes the moment of truth. In the coming days, the American people will learn which politicians are part of the swamp and which politicians want to drain the swamp.

If you make your voices heard and call up your congressmen—and they've been terrific—and call up your senators—and they have been totally terrific. Most of them have been incredible. They really are. They're friends of mine. They've been incredible.

But, it doesn't take much. That's why we need more. We need to have a larger number. But most of them have been incredible. But call your senators. Call your congressmen, because we have no choice. We have to act. We have to act as a country. This isn't good for the Republican Party; this is good for the country and that's ultimately what's it all about.

So, this week, hopefully, the Senate can join the House and take that strong stand for middle-class families and for business, and for jobs, and for competition, and for bringing money back. Together, we will give the American people a big, beautiful Christmas present.

And remember, I was the one—when I was here last time, I said, we're going to have Christmas again. I was the one that said, you go to the department stores and you see "Happy New Years," and you see red, and you see snow, and you see all these things. You don't see "Merry Christmas" anymore.

With Trump as your President, we are going to be celebrating Merry Christmas again, and it's going to be done with a big, beautiful tax cut.

Thank you everybody. God bless you. Thank you. Thank you everybody. Thank you very much.

Even *More* Trump Wins (41-100)

41 Reversing Obama's grab of the Bear's Ears lands
42 The National Security Strategy (December 19th)—America First!
43 Showing Sen. Kirsten Gillibrand of New York how to play big league ball
44 Calling out Sen. Elizabeth "Pocahontas" Warren
45 Recognizing Jerusalem as capital of Israel & moving the Embassy to Jerusalem
46 Limiting refugee settlements in America
47 Re-starting & funding NASA—get to the Moon again & Mars next
48 The rise of Tucker Carlson & Laura Ingraham
49 The implosion of media lefties like Keith Olbermann & Kathy Griffin
50 Vice President & Mrs. Mike Pence—A Model Couple
51 Kellyanne Conway as a face of the Trump Administration
52 Sarah Huckabee Sanders as Press Secretary
53 Calling for an end to the Lottery Visa Program & Chain Migration
54 Encouraging America to buy & hire American
55 Blocking spouses of H-1B Visa Foreign Workers from working while in America
56 Reviewing of all trade agreements to make sure they put America First
57 Seeing "Crooked Hillary" exposed by Bernie Sanders & Donna Brazile
58 Watching the DNC admit that they rigged the Democrat Primary
59 Creating a Commission on Child Trafficking
60 Creating a Commission on Voter Fraud
61 China agreeing to import 90,000 tons of American beef
62 Penalizing Canada for its soft lumber trade cheating
63 Saving almost $100 billion by regulation rollbacks
64 Rolling back regulation to boost coal production & mining
65 Introducing Americans to the world class Mar-a-Lago
66 Getting Jimmy Carter to say nice things & the Bushes to gripe
67 Placing Mick Mulvaney at the head of the Consumer Financial Protection Bureau (& forcing out that Obama bureaucrat)
68 Helping to free the UCLA basketball players from China & calling Lavar Ball a "Poor Man's Don King" for his ingratitude
69 Empowering Dennis Rodman to help make peace with North Korea

70 Giving power to states to drug test unemployment benefit recipients

71 Redirecting the purchase of the next Air Force One to save money

72 Leading the Historic Black College University Initiative

73 Creating an Office for Illegal Immigrant Crime Victims

74 Reversing aspects of Dodd-Frank to stop its draconian regulations

75 Supporting Roy Moore after the media & establishment rushed to judge him

76 Condemning Al Franken after Franken confessed to photo showing assault

77 Pursuing an apprentice program to assist American workers

78 Marking September 3, 2017, as a National Day of Prayer

79 $78 billion promised reinvestment from major businesses like AT&T, Wells Fargo, Fifth Third Bank, Exxon, Bayer, Apple, Softbank & Toyota

80 Denying the FBI a new building that would cost millions when the current building is fine

81 Stopping the elephant hunting via Twitter

82 Achieving the highest manufacturing surge in years

83 Saving $700 million with F-35 plane renegotiation

84 Saving more than $20 Million by reducing White House payroll

85 Negotiating the release of six U.S. humanitarian workers held captive in Egypt

86 Getting Otto Warmbier released from North Korea

87 Being the best U.S. President golfer with a handicap in the low single digits

88 Taking the hopeful & kind visit to Houston after Hurricane Harvey especially when the TV networks covered Trump loading water in cars at relief centers

89 Taking on the mayor of San Juan, a Democrat Hillary supporter, when she was not telling the truth about relief & aid efforts after Hurricane Irma

90 Signed an Executive Order to promote energy independence & economic growth

91 Giving each department head a 6-month time frame dated March 15, 2017, to trim the fat & restructure & improve efficiency of their department & signing an order directing a top-to-bottom audit of the Executive Branch

92 Signing Executive Order establishing Office of Trade & Manufacturing Policy
93 Signing Executive Order expanding offshore drilling
94 Signed Executive Orders to review National Monument designations under prior administrations to decrease Federal land grab
95 Signed Proclamation on Holocaust Remembrance
96 Signed a memo ordering a probe into whether foreign steel is hurting U.S. national security
97 Signed bill allowing states to block Planned Parenthood funding
98 Signed an Order calling for a review of the "Waters Of The United States" Environmental Regulation
99 Signed bill nixing a Social Security Administration rule regarding gun background checks
100 Called for passage of Kate's Law & saw it pass the U.S. House

Acknowledgments and Sources

These are *my* compilation of Trump wins. To come up with this list, I read countless essays and news accounts. I spoke to thousands of people over the past year asking what they saw as Trump wins. There are too many people for me to thank here. However, I must thank this exceptional one: my wife Carol who is the smartest judge of men and politics I know. Her love for me knows no bounds. (Plus, she came up with the title of this book—which Phyllis used to say is "half the book!"). Thank you, Carol. I love you.

I'd like to hear your own Top Trump Wins. Or any disagreements you have with mine. I'm at ed@edmartinlive.com or call/text at (314) 256-1776. Agree, disagree, correct, etc.

For my sources and backup for each Trump Win, please visit edmartinlive.com. The source list will be regularly updated.

About the Author

Ed Martin is the hand-picked successor of Phyllis Schlafly to run her Eagle organizations and currently is President of the Phyllis Schlafly Eagles. He is co-author of the New York Times bestseller *The Conservative Case for Trump* (Regnery, 2016) and currently serves as a commentator on CNN and the host of the Salem Radio network's daily radio show The Ed Martin Movement.

Ed was elected Chairman of the Missouri Republican Party in January 2013 and served on the Republican National Committee until 2015. In 2010, Ed was the Republican nominee for Congress coming within a few thousand votes of beating the incumbent Democrat in the historic Dick Gephardt district. In 2012, Ed was the Republican nomination for Missouri Attorney General while also serving as the Missouri Victor GOTV chairman.

Ed was chief of staff to Missouri Governor Matt Blunt from 2006-2008 helping Missouri leadership pass pro-life legislation, school choice laws, and limiting the reach of the left-wing government unions. In 2005, Ed was appointed Chairman of the St. Louis Board of Election Commissioners. He took the lead in fighting his on ACORN, stream-lined the office, and implemented the Help America Vote Act. In 2006, Ed was the McGivney

Legal Fellow at Americans United for Life and served as lead counsel suing then-Governor Rod Blagojevich for Illinois' imposition on pro-life professionals.

***

Ed holds a law degree and advanced degrees in medical ethics and philosophy and was awarded post-graduate fellowships in Indonesia (Watson Fellowship) and Italy (Rotary Fellowship). After law school, Ed delayed a one year judicial clerkship to serve his church. As the director of the Human Rights Office for the church, Ed led the church community in educating and advocating for pro-life issues, educational opportunities for all, and outreach to the community as part of the new evangelization. It was during this time that Ed learned how Obama-esque "community organizing" was infiltrating our local community; Ed led a successful fight to defund the ACORN-affiliate Missouri Pro-Vote.

Ed spent the summer working at the Institute for Justice in Washington, D.C. assisting on the historic school choice Supreme Court case *Zelman v. Simmons-Harris*. During the 2001-02 term of the federal Court of Appeals for Eighth Circuit, Ed served a judicial clerk to Reagan-appointee Hon. Pasco M. Bowman, II. Immediately following his clerkship, he joined the St. Louis-based international law firm Bryan Cave, LLC specializing in commercial litigation. In the fall of 2004, Ed left Bryan Cave and started his own law firm. He specialized in litigation and small business practice. He was President of the St. Louis Federalist Society and host for the historic Missouri visit of Associate Justice Antonin Scalia in 2004. He has served as executive director of Missouri Club for Growth and founded Missourians United for Life.

***

Ed and his wife Carol, a physician specializing in geriatric internal medicine, reside in St. Louis, Missouri with their two sons and two daughters as well as Lady the boxer.

CPSIA information can be obtained
at www.ICGtesting.com
Printed in the USA
FFOW05n0044100118